Community Activation for Integral Development

As mass global and social media communications spread across the globe, we are seeing a need for a change in the way we approach issues of political and economic development. The effects of these growing communications are that, on the one hand, we see the significance of place rising, while on the other, marginalized people clamour to be heard and identities become increasingly threatened. We are quickly realizing that a 'one-size fits all' approach is not going to work.

Despite more than half a century of attempts to address issues of development, we have seen fairly bleak results. In fact, the rising of economic stars, such as Japan and the Pacific Tigers hitherto, and China and India of late, have little to do with such programs of development or cultural studies, notwithstanding their accomplishment. Typically, such successes have developed top-down, with theories born and bred in the 'West' affecting, or maligning, practices in the 'rest'. The approach taken in this book looks at these developments by turning them on their head: instead, starting *bottom-up* with an emphasis on what the author terms 'community activation'. With a selection of case studies, this volume looks at where community activation can be found and explores how it could evolve and be of use in developing societies at large. In the process, he addresses such topics as how to embed development in a particular society, how to generate social and economic solidarity, and how to generate wealth from pre-industrial and post-industrial networks.

This book provides a guide for readers on how to build community within their organization-and-society from the ground up.

Ronnie Lessem has been an international management consultant in Europe, America, India and Africa for the last three decades.

Transformation and Innovation
Series editors: Ronnie Lessem and Alexander Schieffer

This series on enterprise transformation and social innovation comprises a range of books informing practitioners, consultants, organization developers, development agents and academics how businesses and other organizations, as well as the discipline of economics itself, can and will have to be transformed. The series prepares the ground for viable twenty-first-century enterprises and a sustainable macroeconomic system. A new kind of R & D, involving social, as well as technological innovation, needs to be supported by integrated and participative action research in the social sciences. Focusing on new, emerging kinds of public, social and sustainable entrepreneurship originating from all corners of the world and from different cultures, books in this series will help those operating at the interface between enterprise and society to mediate between the two and will help schools teaching management and economics to re-engage with their founding principles.

For a full list of titles in this series, please visit www.routledge.com/business/series/TANDI

Integral Advantage
Revisiting Emerging Markets and Societies
Ronnie Lessem

Integral Ubuntu Leadership
Passmore Musungwa Matupire

Integral Innovation and Technology Management
A Worldview
Odeh Rashed Al-Jaousi

CARE-ing for Integral Development Series

Volume 1
Community Activation for Integral Development
Ronnie Lessem

Community Activation for Integral Development

Ronnie Lessem

Routledge
Taylor & Francis Group

LONDON AND NEW YORK

First published 2017
by Routledge
2 Park Square, Milton Park, Abingdon, Oxon OX14 4RN

and by Routledge
711 Third Avenue, New York, NY 10017

Routledge is an imprint of the Taylor & Francis Group, an informa business

British Library Cataloguing in Publication Data
A catalogue record for this book is available from the British Library

Library of Congress Cataloging in Publication Data
Names: Lessem, Ronnie, author.
Title: Community activation for integral development / Ronnie Lessem.
Description: New York : Routledge, 2017.
Identifiers: LCCN 2016041396| ISBN 9780415439329 (hardback) |
    ISBN 9781315228730 (ebook)
Subjects: LCSH: Communities. | Sustainable development—
    Social aspects. | Economic development—Technological innovations |
    Economic development—Social aspects.
Classification: LCC HM711 .L47 2017 | DDC 307—dc23
LC record available at https://lccn.loc.gov/2016041396

ISBN: 978-1-138-70124-3 (hbk)
ISBN: 978-1-315-22873-0 (ebk)

Typeset in Times New Roman
by Swales & Willis, Exeter, Devon, UK

Contents

vi *Contents*

Figures

Tables

Prologue
Build community

Introduction

Introducing CARE

Why and for what do we CARE? We care because we, together with and through ourselves as business, community and societal educators and practitioners, social researchers and innovators, altogether in a particular context, seek to develop our collective and institutional world for the better. It is through such CARE that we respectively turn Community activation and collective Awareness raising, institutionalized Research and ultimately Embodying individual and communal, organizational and societal development, into integral, all round, development. With a view to that end, moreover, in Africa, the Middle East and Europe, we are currently engaged in establishing such innovation-driven social research centres, to promote such integral development. Moreover, structurally from the outset, we build community.

In this first of a series of four books on each element of CARE, this particular one focused on community activation for integral development (see Epilogue, especially the grounding tenets for each of the three alternative relational, renewal and realization paths), we seek to amplify your Trans4mative, now collective and institutional as well as individual and communal, journey.

As such, following our previous work on *Integral Renewal: A Relational and Renewal Perspective* (Lessem and Schieffer, 2015), we shall again pursue first, a "southern" *relational* path, as well as second, an "eastern" path of *renewal*, as our primary focus is on the "global south". However, in order to accommodate the rest of the world, at least to some degree, further to our original work on *Integral Research* (Lessem and Schieffer, 2010), where we identified four research paths – southern *relational*, eastern *renewal*, northern *reason* and western *realization* – we also third, pursue a combined "north-western" path of *reasoned realization*. It is for you to choose then, as you did in our previous research works, which path you choose to follow, with a particular focus on grounding and origination in each case.

Technological to social innovation

Three paths of CARE-ing: These three paths – *relational*, *renewal*, *reasoned realization* – altogether, moreover, embody a social, rather than technological, process of research and innovation. After all, Apple Computers, Google, Facebook, if not also Microsoft, are deemed major success stories, building on their technologically based research and development (R & D). Compare this with communities and societies in the African continent, the Indian sub-continent, the Middle Eastern region and South America where success stories are few and far between. So, the conventional wisdom might say, they are in need of "development", or "catch up" with the "west", or now the rising "east". Or alternatively, they are basket cases, disaster zones, rogue states!

Lack of social innovation: When then it comes, on the one collective hand, to such a particular socio-economic community-and-society, be it for example Egypt or Zimbabwe, as opposed to technology based enterprises such as an Apple or a Google, there is no *social R & D*, as such. Sure there are hundreds and thousands of individual students at universities, doing their anthropological, economic, psychological, sociological or business studies "research", as part of their individualized "education", but what has that got to do with releasing the genius of Africa, or India, or Argentina or indeed Syria?

Our collective challenge – CARE: That then is the challenge we have set ourselves at Trans4m Center for Integral Development (Geneva) since the mid 2000s. How do we:

- design collective processes of *Community activation*, while
- purposefully *Awakening* an overall *integral consciousness*,
- promoting *innovation driven institutionalized Research*, and
- ultimately fostering *transformative Education*, if not also *Enterprise*.

All this to CARE for a particular organization/community/society. This we also term our PHD: Process of Holistic Development.

Our individual challenge – 4 Cs: On the other *individual* hand, through a specific PbD (Project-based Development) usually at an undergraduate level, or more general PhD (Doctor of Philosophy) at a postgraduate level, both focused on *integral development* (see definition of "integral worlds" below), we recognize and release a personal as well as societal <u>C</u>alling, set within a particular <u>C</u>ontext, thereby involving <u>C</u>o-creation between social scientific method and content, with a view to making an individual <u>C</u>ontribution to a community, organization and society. However, there are severe limits to what one individual is able to achieve, if our overall aim is to recognize and release the genius of a whole community or society. That is where CARE also comes in.

Our integral rhythm – GENE: What we shall be laying out, in the chapters that follow, is a wide range of integral and developmental perspectives, drawn from all our previous integral work, ranging from *Integral Research* and *Integral Renewal*, to *Integral Enterprise* and *Integral Economics*, to *Integral Community* and *Integral Development, Integral Dynamics and Integral Advantage*, to *Integral Green Zimbabwe* and *Integral Green Slovenia*, to *The Integrators*, each with a particular focus on such <u>C</u>ommunity activation in one respect or another. In the three volumes and respective focus that follows this first one, we do the same for the <u>A</u>wakening of integral consciousness, innovation driven institutionalized <u>R</u>esearch and transformative <u>E</u>ducation, based on the above integral perspectives.

Overall, and in each case here, we pursue the three alternative paths outlined: *relational*, *renewal*, *reasoned realization*. As we pursue CARE, in turn, we follow our integral rhythm, from <u>G</u>rounding (community activation) to <u>E</u>mergence (awakening consciousness) to <u>N</u>avigation (institutionalized research) to <u>E</u>ffect (transformative education and enterprise). Moreover, and holographically so to speak, each CARE part contains the GENE-tic whole. In other words, in community activation as a start, while grounding is your primary focus, this is also with a view to emergence, navigation and effect on one or other of the three alternative paths. Distillations of each path or reality, and trajectory or rhythm, are produced in our Epilogue, as well as in each respective chapter.

Development studies to integral development

Beyond one development size fits all: How does our pursuit of integral development, starting out with community activation, specifically, then relate to development studies, generally? Development studies, cultural studies and hitherto area studies in general, coupled with African-Oriental-Latin American-European Studies specifically, are fields that are burgeoning as our increasingly globalized economies and societies attempt to deal with the backlash of those left behind. Indeed, as globalization and with it mass communications coupled with social media spread remorselessly across the globe, ironically, the significance of local place rises ever more, as marginalized people clamour to be heard (the recent Brexit vote in Britain in the summer of 2016 being a case in point), and identities become increasingly threatened.

As such one-size fits all approaches to political and economic development, as has hitherto been largely the case for development studies, are not very helpful. In fact, and at the extreme, the rise of such destructive, reactive forces across the globe, ranging from ISIS to Boko Haram, are in some respect the result of local identities being crushed or identity crises coming aggressively and reactively to the fore without any integral counterbalance to one-dimensional globalization.

Top down to middle-up-down-across: Despite more than half a century of attempts through area, development or, more recently, cultural studies to address such issues, in Senegal or Saudi Arabia, in Honduras or Haiti, in Greece or in Gambia, the results we see are fairly dismal. In fact, the "home-grown" rising of the economic "tigers", such as Japan and the Pacific Tigers hitherto, and more especially China and India of late, have little connection with such programs of "development studies", more typically aimed at the "global south".

Typically, such studies have developed top-down, with theories born and bred in the "west" affecting, or maligning, practices in the "rest". The approach taken in this book is the opposite to such evolved "middle-up-down-across" so to speak, with approaches to what we first term community activation, born and bred locally in particular societies, with a view to their being further evolved, locally-globally, in developing societies at large.

Towards integral development: In our recent book on *Integral Development* (Schieffer and Lessem, 2013), on which this Prologue most specifically draws, we first introduced what we now term our CARE approach – Community activation, Awakening consciousness, innovation driven institutionalized Research, and ultimately Embodying development. At that stage, we saw each of the four as a part-expression of an altogether would be *integral university*, as a whole. Now we see each one of these as collective constituents of our Process of Holistic Development (PHD). Such a PHD, in fact, accompanies, as mentioned above, either our individual PhD (Doctor of Philosophy) for mature practitioners, or our individual PbD (Project-based Development) for young undergraduate fellows, and/or our OD (Organization Development) for developing organizations. Indeed, each individual PhD, PbD and OD program needs to be contained within our collective oriented PHD focused altogether on CARE.

Underlying all of this, moreover, are what we might call our four integral "design principles", constituting our *integral worlds*. In this opening Prologue, we first outline these, though we shall further elaborate on each in our chapter 5 on releasing GENE-IUS in our second volume on *Awakening Integral Consciousness*. We now outline each so-called integral "design principle", that is our "4 Rs": integral realities, realms, rhythm and rounds.

Integral design principles in brief: 4 Rs

First principle = transcultural Realities: R1
southern, eastern, northern, western

Development, from a transcultural perspective, arises out of particular local realities or worldviews – southern, eastern, northern and western.

To begin with, our orientation towards *transcultural*, as opposed to monocultural, realities serves to root development in particular soils. To that extent, we generally differentiate between *southern* humanism, *eastern* holism, *northern* rationalism and *western* pragmatism, each one of these also having their negative connotations, when part is disconnected from the integral whole (for example, humanism turns into nepotism, pragmatism into materialism). While a particular individual, organization, community or society has the potential to accommodate all such transcultural realities, in terms of both strengths and weaknesses, one or other is likely to dominate in a particular individual, community, organization or society. In this volume, they underlie our three paths.

Moreover, it is precisely in the interaction between local capacities, value bases and developmental orientations on the one hand, and global knowledge, globalized values and development initiatives and needs on the other, that the most impactful processes of research and education, consciousness raising and community activation have taken place. That said, the four design principles, our four Rs, as we shall now see, are highly interdependent, interconnected and integrated ingredients of a new development approach.

Second principle = transdisciplinary Realms: R2
natural, cultural, technological, economic

All integral realms of nature and culture, technology and economy need to be looked at simultaneously and interactively within an all-round integral polity.

Over time, development has been increasingly interpreted as *economic and technological advancement*, and with that came terms like *progress, industrialization* and *modernity*. As a consequence, we overemphasize a limited number of generalized developmental perspectives that are relevant for a particular society, most commonly politically, economically and technologically oriented. What remains relatively marginalized are natural and communal, spiritual and cultural perspectives on such development, which predominate in our relational and renewal paths. While the paths of reason and realization are more outward oriented, universalist and quantifiable, the relational and renewal paths are relatively more inward oriented, particular and qualitative. We distinguish then four major, interconnected realms, altogether constituting an integral polity:

- **economic realm**: economics and enterprise: focus on *realization*;
- **technological realm**: science and technology: focus on *reason*;
- **cultural realm**: humanities and spirituality: focus on *renewal*;
- **natural realm**: ecology and community: *relational* focus.

We now turn to our third, transformational design principle, arguably the most significant for our developmental purposes.

Third principle = Trans4mative Rhythm: R3
grounding, emergence, navigation, effect: GENE

Development, from a transformational perspective, is a rhythmical, dynamic interactive process of grounding (origination) to effect (transformation).

Our third, and probably most significant, *transformational* design principle underlies our research and development rhythm, or integral trajectory, that is from the ground up. In such cyclical and spiralling, as well as linear guise then, the four-fold GENE rhythm, as we shall see in this work, involves altogether:

- *G = Grounding/origination: cyclical/experiential:* Call/Community *activation*

    You are locally *grounded* in a particular organization and/or community, as we shall later see for example in Chinyika, Zimbabwe, or in Edo State, Nigeria, in response to your inner, and its outer *call*, with a view to collective *community activation*, following a relational, renewal or realization path.
- *E = Emergent foundation: spiralling/imaginative:* Context and Awakening

    Moving towards local-global *emergence* locates you and your organization/community in an evolving context, whereby you are individually interpreting the imbalances therein, with a view to alleviating them. This altogether and thereafter ultimately requires, of yourselves collectively, an *awakening of integral consciousness*, again in relational, renewal or realization guise. However, and with an initial view to such, we incorporate the full integral rhythm from the *community activation* at the outset.

- *N = Emancipatory navigation: linear/conceptual:* Co/creation/Research

  The move to *navigation* requires that the experiences gained and new insights acquired are translated by you individually into new concepts, new knowledge, new technologies, new institutions, through *co-creation* between science and society. This now assumes newly global, or universal, proportions. Thereafter, once again collectively in "southern" relational, "eastern" renewal or "north-western" realization terms, requires the development of innovation-driven, institutionalized Research.

- *E = Transformative effect: point/practical:* Contribution/Education-Enterprise

  Moving to *effect* finally now requires you to put all prior three of the above into integrated, altogether transformative *Education* and/or *Enterprise*. It is about pragmatically and economically applying the new knowledge that has been developed, thereby actualizing the research and innovation that it contains, thus making an individual contribution to your organization and/or society, and collectively transforming education and/or enterprise, on a duly relational, renewal and/or realization path.

We now come finally to our fourth design principle, which earmarks our approach to individual and organizational, societal and world (universal) development, altogether.

Fourth principle = transpersonal Rounds: R4
individual, organizational, societal, universal

All development levels – self, organization, society, and universe – need to be holistically and interactively included ("fully rounded").

Finally, we argue that the conventional discourse on development is primarily held at a generalized societal level, as well as, partly, on a community level. Usually not included are the *transpersonal* levels of individual development, at school and at university, and organizational, development, in-house and through external consultancy, alongside community and societal development, altogether in a particular context. We advocate, as part of this fourth and final design principle, the following four interconnected levels, or integral rounds, and to look at them within any given development context:

- *level 1/round 1*: self-development (self and other);
- *level 2/round 2*: organizational development (group and organization);
- *level 3/round 3*: societal development (community and society);
- *level 4/round 4*: universal development (world).

Besides recognition of all levels – from self to world – it is also important to look at each level in a holistic or *rounded* way. That now brings us directly to our overall, collective process of CARE-ing for integral and rounded – thereby inclusive of individual, communal, organizational and societal – development, as we shall see: Communal activation, Awakening consciousness, Research and innovation, transformative Education. We start in this book with community activation, via alternately relational, renewal and reasoned realization paths, each also with its own integral rhythm or trajectory. As such, holographically as we have said, the CARE whole is contained within, or anticipated by, the community activation part. As such, CARE is differentiated and integrated.

Collective CARE-ing: relational, renewal and realization paths

Communal activation: alongside inner and outer individual calling

Collectively based communal activation then – paralleling an individual's inner and outer calling – is covered in this current volume (see Table 0.1) with a particular focus on grounding, but also with a view to emergence, navigation and effect for each respective path, thereby including the integral rhythm from grounding (origination) to emergence foundation) onto navigation (emancipation) and ultimately effect (transformation).

In Table 0.1, we provide an initial overview on core aspects of such community activation, which will be expanded upon in this book.

Table 0.1 CARE

Grounding: Communal activation: livelihood, healing, truth quest relational, renewal, reasoned-realization paths from ubuntu ("I am because you are") to group individuation

- *Integrator role*: community integrator, e.g. Chidara Muchineripi, Chinyika, Zimbabwe; Father Anselm Adodo/Pax Herbals, Nigeria; Louis Herman, Future Primal, South Africa/Ancient Greece.
- *Communal function*: secure livelihoods (relational), heal communities (renewal) or pursue truth quest (reasoned realization) through which communities restore, recreate or actualize their full potential.

Community activation/awakening integral consciousness

Awakening integral consciousness, now locally-globally, in other words emerging from the ground up albeit in association with others, which is anticipated in this current work on CARE, but followed more fully in our second volume on CARE – running parallel to individual context – again follows a relational path, a path of renewal and of reasoned realization, each characterized by an integral rhythm, now with a particular focus on indigenous-exogenous emergence. Such a developmental mode transcends the level of an individual, organization and community and has its main focus on integral consciousness raising, of self and community, organization and society, altogether. Indeed, it acts as a veritable catalyst for the evolution of such and thereby taps strongly into the cultural and spiritual sources of a polity as a whole. In that process, it renews the culture and spirit of each and contributes to the "regeneration of meaning". In this current work, as an emergent expression of community activation, it is manifested as shown in Table 0.2.

Community activation and awakening of integral consciousness aligned with innovation-driven institutionalized research/innovation

We now turn from community activation and awakening of integral consciousness to now, and newly, and globally oriented, innovation-driven research, initially covered here CARE-wise, and more fully articulated in a third volume on fully fledged CARE. Here you build on local community activation and the local-global awakening of integral consciousness that has come before.

Integrally reframed, innovation driven, institutionalized social *research* represents now newly, and globally oriented social science, inclusive of the life sciences and the humanities, collectively set alongside individual

Table 0.2 CARE

Emergence: Community activation/Awaken integral consciousness relational, renewal, reasoned realization paths of integral awakening earth justice to history making

- *Integrator role*: development integrator, e.g. Mollinson, Australia (relational); Escobar, Columbia (renewal); Flores, Chile (realization).
- *Integrative function*: permaculture (relational); vitality of place (renewal); disclosing new worlds (reasoned realization) through which communities reclaim, revitalize or actualize their full potential.

co-creation of science and society. It is focused, building on community activation and consciousness raising, on scholarship, research and knowledge creation aiming – simultaneously – for technological but more particularly social innovation (see Table 0.3).

Social sciences, for us as such, take precedence over the natural sciences – and the humanities are restored to their rightful place alongside social and natural sciences. Knowledge is not regarded as static, but as continuously, dynamically unfolding. We finally turn to transformative education.

Community activation aligned with awakening consciousness, institutionalized research and embodied development

Embodied development now builds on community activation, awakening integral consciousness and institutionalized research, though communal grounding continues to occupy pride of place here. Fully fledged embodied development comes into play then in our volume four. This embodies practical, now globally-local *facilitation*. It involves creative experimentation, as we will see in the Grameen case (Chapter 11) and is a conducive space in which new individual, organizational and societal practices can be conceived of, tested and implemented, as indeed was the case for the Grameen Bank in Bangladesh.

It represents new ways of learning and mirrors the growing desire for developmental-educational spaces that deal, hands on, through action learning and action research with the burning issues societies are facing, drawing also on the individual and collective capacities therein. Moreover, it builds on the community activation, awakening of integral consciousness, and innovation driven institutionalized research that has come before, the first of these having pre-emphasis in this current work (see Table 0.4).

Table 0.3 CARE

Navigation: community activation/awaken integral consciousness/innovation-driven institutionalized Research relational, renewal, realization paths to innovative social science decoloniality to wealth of networks
• *Integrator role*: Pundutso Centre Zimbabwe (relational); CISER – Centre for Social and Economic Research Nigeria (renewal); and Citizen's Initiative for Integral Green Slovenia (realization), locally, all together with Trans4m Center (globally). • *Innovative function*: participatory research (relational); study circles (renewal), wealth of networks (reasoned realization).

Table 0.4 CARE

Effect: Embodying development in community activation, awakening consciousness, institutionalized research relational, renewal to realization paths to rebuild human capacity grounding to effecting individual and collective potential

- *Integrator role*: Cashbuild, South Africa (relational); Grameen, Bangladesh (renewal); and Nizhnii Novgorod, Russia (realization).
- *Transformative function*: communal building (relational); self-sufficiency (renewal); purveyors of the province (reasoned realization).

Conclusion: where do we go from here?

Functional complementarity

The following applies to all four CARE functions outlined:

- Each can serve to complement, if not altogether reform the existing educational system of an organization or society.
- Each is primarily an authentic articulation of, first, one particular reality or worldview (southern, eastern, northern, western); second, a specific realm or discipline (natural, cultural, technological, economic); third, applied to successive rounds (self, organization, society, world); ultimately following an integral rhythm (grounding, emergence, navigation, effecting).
- As we shall see in the chapters that follow, each thereby carries to some degree the other CARE functions within itself.

If we look at it from an evolutionary perspective, we see all four functions as authentic, but partial expressions of a larger, not yet fully visible totality. In other words, we envision the full integration of community activation, awakening of consciousness, innovation driven institutionalized research and transformative education into a fully "integral university". This is the task that faces us, spread across all four volumes of CARE.

Community activation: three paths and fourfold rhythm

Community activation then, as will be the case for all four CARE functions, has three alternative paths you can follow, being southern *relational*, eastern *renewal* and the combined though less travelled in our own integral case (because of our particular focus on the global south) north-western path of *reasoned realization* (Figure 0.1).

SCIENTIFIC NAVIGATION
EMANCIPATION
Build Up Social Capital (S)
Animated Community (E)
Open Source (N/W)

ECONOMIC EFFECT   CARE   CULTURAL EMERGENCE
TRANSFORMATION   *INTEGRATION*   *FOUNDATION*
Community Building (S)   *Community*   *Permaculture (S)*
Self sufficiency (E)   *Activation/*   Vitality of Place (E)
Mutual Development (N/W)   **Relational/Renewal/**   Disclosive Worlds (N/W)
Reasoned Realization
Research Paths/Realities

NATURAL GROUNDING
ORIGINATION
Securing Livelihoods (S)
Healing Community (E)
Truth Quest (N/W)

Figure 0.1 CARE paths/rhythm: relational, renewal, realization.

Specifically, the southern path is in italics, the eastern one in plain type and the north-western one underlined, each one to be followed anti-clockwise, that is south-east-north-west. Each GENE-tic part of the integral trajectory then, for each of the three paths, has four key tenets, as well as an overall core tenet, attached to it, as we shall see.

We now turn to grounding community activation on the respectively "southern" relational path, and thereafter to the "eastern" path of renewal and then "north-western" reasoned realization. Such grounded community activation specifically, by way of a poignant example, draws on developmental programs and processes with which we have been significantly concerned for a decade, in Zimbabwe in Southern Africa, in Nigeria in West Africa, and in South Africa via Hawaii. We turn first, locally and communally, to Zimbabwe, whereby we shall focus initially on the "southern" relational grounding of the path of community activation and its five particular, collective research tenets.

As ultimately highlighted in our concluding Epilogue, it is invariably, for each path, the grounding and origination that sets the underlying tone. What follows, GENE-tically, and if you like holographically, connects with CARE as a whole. While then such CARE (community activation) is your and our reason for being in this first volume in our quartet focused in particular on integral realities, CARE (awakening integral consciousness) oriented especially toward our integral rhythm, CARE (innovation-driven institutionalized research) focused in particular in integral realms and

CARE (embodying integral development) especially oriented towards integral rounds then respectively follow suit, in all cases both part and whole being manifest. We start, for our relational grounding, with Chinyika, lodged within a "southern" reality, in Zimbabwe, remembering that our purpose here is not merely to write four books but to co-evolve relevant integral research centres.

References

Lessem, R. and Schieffer, A. (2010) *Integral Research and Innovation*. Abingdon, UK: Routledge.

Lessem, R. and Schieffer, A. (2015) *Integral Renewal: A Relational and Renewal Perspective*. Abingdon, UK: Routledge.

Schieffer, A. and Lessem, R. (2013) *Integral Development: Realizing the Transformative Potential of Individuals, Organizations and Societies*. Abingdon, UK: Routledge.

Part I

Southern grounding of community

Livelihood, healing, truth quest

1   Securing livelihoods

Grounding of the relational path

A natural-communal perspective on community activation

Summary of chapter:

1   underpinned by ubuntu ("I am because you are");
2   adding natural and communal value;
3   building up social capital organizationally and/or communally-societally;
4   culminating in common ownership;
5   centred in the securing of livelihoods.

Orientation: securing livelihoods

Care and CARE

In our focus on *community activation,* via different integral perspectives portrayed through our *integral rhythm* (see Table 1.1), we start with local grounding (G), our major pre-emphasis, and then proceed through local-global emergence (E), global navigation (N) and global-local effect (E), herein via Chinyika in Zimbabwe, albeit that Community activation remains primary (Care), albeit in integral (CARE) guise. First, we focus on grounding and origination of the now collective "southern" (S) *relational* path, which occupies pride of relational place, the pre-emphasis here being *securing livelihoods*. Indeed, each part of the integral rhythm also contains, as we shall see, the whole GENE.

As already illustrated, the *relational* path of *community activation* focuses GENE-tically on: livelihoods (G); natural/communal value (E); social capital (N); and common ownership (E). Our opening "southern" *relational* case in point, with a particular focus on securing livelihoods, is Chinyika in rural Zimbabwe (Figure 1.1).

Table 1.1 Relationally grounded rhythm of natural CARE

Grounded communal activation: livelihood southern relational path and trajectory restores livelihood through nature and community

- *Communal relational integral rhythm*: grounding – livelihood, healing, truth quest; emergence – permaculture, vitality of place, disclosing new worlds; navigation – participatory, study circles, networks; effect – community building, self-sufficiency, mutual aid.
- *Integrator role*: community steward, e.g. Dr Paul Muchineripi, Chinyika.
- *Communal function*: communal learning and development through which communities reclaim their source of livelihood.
- *Grounded in livelihood*: *ubuntu* provides the original ground and the purpose; naturally based value is the foundational source of emergent contribution; social capital is the emancipation of community; effectively and transformatively leading to a common ownership; at best such communities make a powerful socio-economic contribution to society; at worst patriarchy/ethnicity/partisan politics prevails.

The GENE-ius of community

Community activation is the first of our four CARE functions: to be followed in future volumes by fully fledged, awakening integral consciousness, innovation driven institutionalized research, and finally by transformative education.

We now turn to our specific and opening case of such community activation, that of Chinyika in rural Zimbabwe. Following an overall "southern" *relational* path through such communal activation, we shall pursue an integral *rhythm* or trajectory through local grounding and origination, a local-global emergent foundation, a newly global emancipation, and ultimately a global-local effect. We start with our local *relational* grounding

TENET LG 3
Build Social Capital (S)

TENET LG4	CORE TENET	TENET LG 2
Common Ownership (S)	**Secure Livelihoods**	*Add Natural Value (S)*
	e.g. Muchineripi/Chinyika/Zimbabwe	

TENET LG 1
Underlying Ubuntu (S)

Figure 1.1 Relational community activation: grounding tenets.

of and through Chinyika in Zimbabwe, with the overall object in this case of *securing livelihoods*.

Setting the Zimbabwean stage

Founding ancestors

In this opening chapter on *munhu/ubuntu* (I am because you are) mediated through Chinyika, a rural community in Zimbabwe, we show how, through activating the participation of especially women (as part of their PhD/ PHD – Process of Holistic Development – program, with Trans4m and Da Vinci Institute), Dr Chidara Muchineripi and Dr Steve Kada were able to engage their Chinyika community in taking charge of their individual and communal lives.

As such, they collectively changed a negative situation of hunger and starvation into a positive one of food security and self-sufficiency. In fact, it is Chinyika which set the initial, rural and communal stage for what we have termed *Integral Green Zimbabwe* to follow (Mamukwa *et al.*, 2014).

What then is such a southern communal impetus in this illustrative case in Zimbabwe, starting indeed from the ground up, which we liken to a phoenix rising from the ashes of its recent troubled history? The Chinyika story from rural Zimbabwe is grounded in nature and community (Lessem *et al.*, 2012). The authentic development of Zimbabwe rests in the hands of neither international capitalists nor communists, but rather, as we shall see, in a local identity, duly evolving towards a global integrity. Indeed, for UK based leading African historian, Basil Davidson, in his book on *African Genius* (Davidson, 1969), the history of the Africans is nothing if not the "handing on the torch" from generation to generation. It is quintessentially concerned with the accumulation of ancestral wisdom. For it is the appointed ancestors who have given peoples their identity and guaranteed the onward movement of life. They may be private ancestors or public ancestors, family guarantors or national guarantors, but in any case, their role is crucial. In Zimbabwe, the Shona peoples think of their great ancestral spirits, the *mhondoro*, who, as founding heroes, first taught them how to smelt iron from the rocks and how to grow millet and sorghum.

It was in this sense that spiritual belief systems lay at the heart of the local Shona people in Zimbabwe. One specific group, the Karanga, was prominently represented by Muchineripi (Paul "Chidara" Muchineripi), as the son of the Chinyika rural Chief. Chidara was also a business consultant in urban Harare and is now a Doctor of Philosophy. The other key representative in our communal story was Baremba-based Steve Kada, as a Human Resource Director of a leading Zimbabwean food processing company, and now also Dr Kada. As respective Chinyika community activators, their role, together with significant others, was to "connect themselves" with those ancestors to whom super-sensible power had revealed the land and shown Muchineripi and Kada how to prosper.

Chinyika project of community activation

Poverty rooted in colonial history

For Muchineripi and Kada, the colonization of Zimbabwe (as Rhodesia) had the profoundly debilitating effect of an imposed and dominant "western" conventional economic system. From 1890, the country was subjected to restructuring according to exogenous "western" or indeed "northern" thinking and the exogenous economic philosophies that prevailed. The indigenous communities under the dominant colonial system were shaken from their cultural roots. The country evolved into a newly colonial political and economic system, thereby falling under exogenous, crudely capitalist sway.

Wake up call: a son-to-be-steward was raised from the house of Gutu

Paul "Chidara", a son-to-be-steward, was raised from the house of the Gutu chieftainship out of the Chinyika community and was moved by the suffering of his own people. He woke up to the call of his ancestors to save his people from the scourge of hunger and poverty. Chidara, having become a successful business person and management educator, had a wakeup call from his retrospective slumber of individual success. Early in the new millennium, prompted initially by his participation in a Masters program in social and economic transformation run by Trans4m (Geneva) in South Africa, accredited by Buckingham University in the UK (his initial motivation to participate in the Masters program was to improve himself as a manager), and hosted by the so called CIDA (Community and Individual Development in Africa) City Campus, he ultimately responded to his "father's voice".

Awareness gripped him and reminded him, while he was looking after his own individual interests, also of his collective responsibility to his own people, representing his and their inner and outer "calling" so to speak, as the son of a chief. Emotively aroused, he (together with his wife Nakirai) initially decided to feed the people who were starving in Chinyika by buying bags of mealie meal (corn) and grain, and distributing them.

While in the process of facing this challenge and responding to his "father's voice" to take care of his people, he enrolled on the Trans4m Masters Program in Social and Economic Transformation (MSET) in 2005, unknowingly together with his comrade in adversity Steve Kada. That was the beginning of their move to Community. He (Chidara) then reconnected with the voice that called his people – an "outer call" – to revisit the source of their food security in the past, the nutritious food and meals that came out of the sweat of their labour, the original source of their livelihoods.

The primacy of finger millet: the transformation journey

The outer call was echoed through poems and drama. One villager, at a "field day" (where farmers exhibited their produce) inspiringly recited the poem:

> The grass that turns into gold
> The grass that gives people their livelihood
> The grass that is fed to people and their livestock
> The grass that connects the Chinyika people with the ancestral spirits
> The grass that acts as a medium between the people and the spirits
> The grass that has value beyond money
> The grass that makes and gives life to people
> The grass that derives its life from the soil but also gives back to the soil
> the nutrients that nourishes the soil.

The poem summarizes the value and the importance of finger millet, one of the "key natural actors", as it were, for the Chinyika people.

The Golden grain, rapoko, was going to play a critical role in their communal transformation journey. It would be at the centre of all their activities in developing food security in the Chinyika households. Through this re-visitation of the past, Chidara reconnected with the tradition and culture of growing indigenous small grains. For him, the voice of his father had always echoed throughout his lifetime. At the same time, his mother, while she was alive, had not abandoned the clan's cultural farming norms, and she remained a custodian and implementer of the traditional grain growing and food preparation, which would indeed become a lifeline to the Chinyika Community. She was a typical African mother of her community, and more of such, as we shall see, was to come.

After becoming co-researchers, Chidara and Steve then spent endless hours together in Chidara's special gazebo thatched structure, while they participated part-time together on the Masters at his home in Harare. He was filled with great emotion as he narrated the story of his village people, promoted by the reminder, through his education and research, of his grounding. He would clench his fists, put his hands on each side of his body and stamp the ground as if in a dance. It was as if he were planting himself in the soil of his ancestors as he rooted himself in the centre and soul of Chinyika's traditional past. His father, as a chief, had passed on the oral tradition of a true African to his family and subjects, "A true African does not completely abandon his culture despite getting a western education. Western education has its virtues but the African has to maintain his humane nature".

Chief Chitsa of Chinyika, in addressing people on one of the field days said, "Munhu ega ega, mwana ega ega anofanira kuziva kwaakabva" translated as: "Each person, each child must look back and know where they came from and be responsible to himself and his community like what we have witnessed today. Our son Chidara has demonstrated that each one of us must be responsible to their people".

Public-private-civic partnership

Chidara was born near Chinyika rock (Figure 1.2). Chidara representing the Chinyika community in his capacity as designate chief, and Steve representing the business sector as HR Director of Cairns Foods, played their respective roles in activating the community. As such, they created a relationship between the private sector and the rural community, with the Zimbabwean Department of Agriculture ultimately also playing its governmental part.

On the one hand, Cairns Foods, through their agronomists, provided the Chinyika community with technical advice in growing the traditional and horticultural crops. On the other, the Chinyika people provided Cairns Foods with a wealth of knowledge for the purposes of product development. Cairns, in its own transformation process, was turning towards foods with a traditional base and flavour in addition to the current western oriented food products on the market.

At that time, Cairns was in fact producing western products like wines, cornflakes, breakfast jams and tinned vegetables. Thereafter, through its newly constituted research and development team, it evolved a product prepared from small grains, specifically sorghum and rapoko. The urban African elite was now turning to more traditionally based products like porridges, peanut butter, and organically grown crops. A market opportunity for traditional small grains like rapoko, peanuts and pumpkins was slowly emerging. Through the private sector, production of these high nutrient content foods, together with communities like Chinyika, resulted.

At the same time, the government sponsored agricultural extension officers hailed the reintroduction of rapoko on a greater scale than before.

Figure 1.2 The Chinyika rock.

Note: Chidara's mother's kitchen where he was born was between the two rocks to the east. His father's grave is also to the east of the rock.

Together, they revisited the traditional knowledge base of growing rapoko and the preparation of the delicious meals that the people were now enjoying.

Musha ndimai: towards a democratic community

Through the re-awakening that had been taking place among the Chinyika community, as well as in neighbouring communities – extending from 5,000 people in 2006 to up to 300,000 in 2013 – individual effort was being channelled and realized in the context of communal benefit. Such practical realization was encouraged to the extent that it did not create selfish egoistic individuals. The unifying force between the individual and the community was the focus on fighting the resurgence of food insecurity and the continued battle against poverty to realize the capacity and strength that the people have in growing enough food and to alleviate poverty.

In order to coordinate these developments, the leadership originally drew from the villages' horizontal structures. Through a democratic process in the traditional manner, the Chief, headman, counsellors, village development committees, extension services personnel were all involved, consulted and contributed to the selection of the project leadership. The leadership, headed by Mai Mlambo (Mrs Mlambo), who had been appointed by the Chinyka villagers as head of their Community Council, had clearly outlined their goals and strategy specifically to fight hunger through growing rapoko and in the long run eliminating poverty. They had meanwhile clearly distanced themselves from the very sensitive partisan politics. They did not therefore align the project farming activities with any political groupings. The committees' main purpose remained that of building a community consciousness that creates enlightened peoples' actions to fight both mind and material poverty; to thereby decolonize the mind.

In the process of putting together the project leadership, the role of a woman had been re-defined. Mothers had awoken to take up their traditional role – the home stands because of the mother – "Musha ndimai", and duly evolved it.

Conclusion: releasing the GENE-ius of Chinyika

Auto-centric development

The ultimate effect, at first for 5,000 and ultimately seven years later for up to 300,000 villagers, was the realization of food security in economic terms and of an evolved polity in socio-political terms, combining tradition with modernity. As such, there has been the auto-centric development of a village democracy, where nature and community generally, and women – natural and communal mothers – occupied pride of place. Indeed, all of this arose despite, rather than because of, national politics, which were purposefully kept out of this natural and communal process.

Community activation: relational path/integral rhythm

Of course the result has been that such an integral polity at Chinyika, born out of nature and culture, society and economy, is not evident on a national stage. In effect, Zimbabwe in particular and Africa in general has not yet risen, nationally and regionally, to the "southern" integral occasion, because such community activation has not been the starting or indeed end point. To the extent that it was and is, underlying ubuntu, the adding of natural value, the build up of social capital and the development of community ownership, together serving to secure livelihoods, would be the "southern" relational route to follow.

Where then do we go from here as community activators? And where does Zimbabwe go from here, to become *Integral Green Zimbabwe* or some such, uniquely and thereby auto-centrically its own? Therein lies its work in progress, to be followed up in our future volumes. But we now turn from the grounding of the "southern" relational path to the origination of the "eastern" path of renewal, that is to integral healing in Nigeria to progress the story of community activation in Africa, both culturally and spiritually.

References

Davidson, B. (1969) *The African Genius.* New York: Atlantic Monthly Press.
Lessem, R., Muchineripi, P. and Kada, S. (2012) *Integral Community: Political Economy to Social Commons.* Farnham, UK: Gower.
Mamukwa, E., Lessem, R. and Schieffer, A. (2014) *Integral Green Zimbabwe.* Abingdon, UK: Routledge.

2 Healing community

Grounding of the eastern path of renewal

A Pax Africana perspective on community activation

Summary of chapter:

1   underpinned by nature power;
2   furthered through fusing work and prayer;
3   consolidated upon by combining nature, spirit, science, economy;
4   ultimately establishing communitalism within your organization/society;
5   centred in community healing.

Introduction: healing pre-emphasis

Healing individuals and communities

We continue to ground community activism in African soils, this time via the "eastern" path of renewal (Figure 2.1), especially relevant for those pursuing the path of renewal grounded in *Individual and Communal Healing,* turning from Chinyika in Zimbabwe to Paxherbals in Nigeria, and thereby to Dr Father Anselm Adodo (Lessem, 2016) as a *communal integrator.* In fact, Father Anselm, suitably inspired by the Chinyika case, made a special trip to Zimbabwe to see it first hand. While on the one hand he was duly inspired by this grass-roots case of community activation, on the other he was struck by the comparative lack of a spirit of renewal underlying this communal (Care) impulse compared to his own at Paxherbals emerging into Pax Africana. Who then is Anselm Adodo, and what set him on the road to communal activation in Nigeria, and how does his approach to healing community connections differ from that of securing livelihoods, albeit remaining true to "southern" grounding?

Anselm Adodo (Adodo, 2016) was born on 2 November 1969, in the serene environment of a modern government hospital in Akure, the capital of Ondo State, Western Nigeria. No fuss. No complication. Just the normal

TENET NG3
Combining Nature, Spirit, Science, Economy (E)

TENET NG4   *CORE TENET NG*   TENET NG2
Communitalism (E)   **Heal Community**   *Fusing Work and Prayer (E)*
                        e.g. Adodo/Pax/Nigeria

TENET NG1
Nature Power (E)

Figure 2.1 Renewed community activation: grounding tenets.

birth of an ordinary child on a normal day. A few hundred miles away, war was raging in Eastern Nigeria; the Nigerian civil war, in which one million lives were lost. It was a war between the Igbo tribe, one of the largest ethnic groups in Nigeria, who had declared secession from the Nigeria nation-state. Nigeria, a concoction of different ethnic tribes, is, according to Adodo, an artificial creation of the British colonial power, as indeed Rhodesia (now Zimbabwe) had been. Forcing together the diverse tribes that made up this vast geographical space under one umbrella was a convenient way for the British government to exercise control and governance.

The Biafra war lasted from July 1967 to January 1970. It ended three months after Anselm was born. A few hundred miles away, in the eastern part of Nigeria, hundreds of thousands of new born children were dying of starvation, families displaced, and hopes shattered. It was a sharp contrast to the serenity of the environment from which he emerged. Adodo later grew up to read about this war and its atrocities in the history books, himself growing up in a peaceful household.

Searching for knowledge and monastic community

Anselm was born in a modern hospital, to a father who was a school principal and science teacher, critical of "unproven, old-fashioned" traditions, to a mother who was also a school teacher. She was a devout Christian whose Christian faith called some traditional fetish practices into question. Meanwhile his grandmother and grandfather were believers in tradition but not to the point of fanaticism or foolishness.

Anselm's first school was a Catholic boy's college, famed for discipline, high academic standards and excellence in sports. Anselm was indeed fascinated by the world of biology, chemistry, mathematics and physics. He could but marvel at the intricate complexity of the amoeba, the sophistication of the human heart and its incessant rhythm, the intricate complexity of the human brain, and the laws of physics and chemistry. He also wondered at the audacity with which these laws were stated, as if they were infallible. Meanwhile, unbeknown to his father, Anselm had, along with two of his friends, paid an exploratory visit to a catholic monastery in Edo State, where a group of monks lived, worked and prayed. They interacted with the monks and spent some four days with them. Anselm had read about such monks and how they often were compared with mad people, due to the illogical and strange nature of their way of life. In November 1987, he abandoned his university admission and joined the monastery.

St. Benedict comes to Edo State

Perched on a hill one thousand feet above sea level, St. Benedict monastery was founded by a group of Irish missionary monks, with the aim of spreading the monastic tradition to West Africa. They chose Edo State, geographically located right in the middle of Nigeria, linking the north, east, west and south. Today, the St. Benedict Monastery is of one of the most culturally diverse monastic communities in Africa, representing 15 different ethnic groups in Nigeria. In fact, in his study of philosophy, Anselm was fascinated by the unending search of human beings from different traditions, cultures, races and religions for *truth*.

Towards Paxherbals

What is a monastery?

In 2004, after 17 years of living in a Benedictine Monastery as a monk, Adodo, by now Father Anselm Adodo, had to edit a book that told the story of the St. Benedict Monastery, as part of the celebration to mark the silver jubilee of the existence of the monastic community of Ewu. In the book titled *The Story of Ewu Monastery: Silver Jubilee Reflections* (2004) he wrote:

> Monastic life did not start in the desert lands of Egypt, or in the fertile green farms of Canaan, or in the Garden of Eden. Monastic life did not originate in the high mountains of the Himalayas, or on the holy mount of Horeb. Monastic life originated in the human heart. It started the moment God, the almighty and all powerful said: I am one, let me be many.

What sort of man: monk, priest, scholar, herbalist

There was a full-page write up in the *Guardian Newspaper* of January 2003, one of Nigeria's elite newspapers and arguably the most respected Nigerian daily. The article is titled: "Monk who heals with herbs". The paper featured the picture of a man dressed in traditional and Western attire, looking like a traditional native doctor and Western physician at the same time. The picture was captioned "what sort of man?"

The article was about a Catholic priest who was also an herbalist, Christian theologian and a social scientist. It was a tribute to the uniqueness of what Father Adodo was doing: creating synergy, so to speak between "south" (nature), "east" (spirit), "north" (truth) and "west" (enterprise) (Table 2.1). It also hinted at the paradox of a Catholic priest belonging to a highly conservative order who dedicated himself to the promotion of traditional medicine. It was the paradox of a man engaged in fusing indigenous with exogenous knowledge, and the editor of the newspaper must have wondered, like many other observers, what sort of a man this was? Combining both the indigenous and the exogenous is certainly a challenging task.

His goal was to change the face of African traditional medicine

Anselm had returned from America eight years before in 1996, armed with a Bachelor's Degree in Religious Studies and a Masters in Systematic Theology from Duquesne University of the Holy Ghost, Pittsburgh, USA.

Table 2.1 Grounded CARE for communitalism

Grounding communal activation: individual and communal healing eastern path of renewal healing community with a view to communitalism
• *Communal attributes*: grounding – livelihoods, healing, truth quest; emergence – permaculture, vitality, new worlds; navigation – participatory, study circles, networks; effect – community building, self-sufficiency, mutual advantage.
• *Integrator role*: community steward, e.g. Dr Father Anselm Adodo/ *Paxherbals*.
• *Communal function*: individual and communal healing.
• *Grounded in value*: *Local-global value* provides the ground and the overall purpose that of *harnessing nature power*; provides for ongoing fusion of prayer (*ora*) and work (*labore*); navigates through combining nature, spirit, science, economy in the overall context of *Pax Africana*; ultimately practising communitalism; at their best such communities are characterized by a contributing to society spiritually and economically; at their worst rigid dogma prevails.

He was immediately recruited to teach the phenomenology of religion, theology and sociology of religion, as well as comparative religion, in a nearby catholic seminary where priests were trained. At the same time, he was given the post of the monastery's bursar. The burning issue for the monastery then was how to become economically self-sufficient and stop depending on aid from the parent house in Ireland for its survival.

At the same time, in Edo State, there were traditional healers everywhere, and traditional shrines could be sited in many corners of the village. There was a mission hospital and a government hospital in the village, but the majority of the people also patronized traditional healers. At the time, herbal medicine was identified with witchcraft, sorcery, ritualism and all sorts of fetish practices. Because herbal medicine was associated with paganism, African-Christians patronized traditional healers, in secret, and the educated elite and religious figures did not want to be associated in any way with traditional African medicine.

Moreover, for a religious figure, especially a catholic priest like Father Anselm, to be openly propagating traditional medicine was seen as a taboo of the highest order. In fact, his goal was to change the face of African traditional medicine. Four years later, in 2000, Anselm Adodo's book titled *Nature Power. A Christian Approach to Herbal Medicine* was published (Adodo, 2012).

There were in fact for him two approaches to herbal medicine practice, namely the clinic-oriented approach and the community-oriented approach. In a clinic-oriented approach, emphasis is placed on scientific identification, conservation and use of medicinal plants. Laboratory research and screening are done to determine the chemical composition and biological activities of plants. Great interest is shown in quality control of raw materials and finished products, and development of methods for large scale production of labelled herbal drugs. The herbal drugs are labelled and packaged in the same way as modern drugs and distributed through similar channels, that is, through recognized health officials in hospitals, health centres or pharmaceutical supply chains. Huge sums of money are invested by the government, private companies and non-governmental organizations to promote further research into herbal medicine. Minimal interest is shown in the socio-cultural use of the plants.

In the community-oriented approach, the emphasis is on the crude and local production of herbs used for common illnesses. Knowledge of the medicinal uses of herbs is spread to promote self-reliance. Information is freely given on disease prevention and origin of diseases. This approach aims at applying simple but effective herbal remedies to common illnesses. The target is the local community. No interest is shown in mass production of drugs for transportation to other parts of the country or exportation to other countries. The cultural context of the plants used is taken into account, and local perception of health and healing often takes precedence over modern diagnostic technology. Simple Herbal recipes are used for the treatment of such illnesses as coughs, colds, malaria and typhoid. The two approaches analysed above are two extremes. There was a need to harmonize these two extremes to complement each other. Paxherbals was established in 1996. It was registered as a private liability company and in 2002 was described as "a Catholic research centre for scientific identification, conservation, utilization and development of African medicinal plants".

Paxherbals to communitalism: towards Pax Africana

Community activation to awakening integral consciousness

Some 15 years later, inspired by his participation in Trans4m's PhD/PHD program, Anselm took a next step, turning Paxherbals towards Pax Afrikana (see also Figure 2.2):

- to serve as a centre for genuine African holistic healing that blends the physical and the spiritual aspects of the human person;
- to become a model comprehensive health care centre where the western (north, west) and traditional (south, east) systems of healing are creatively blended;
- to be an example of how proper utilization of traditional medicine can promote grassroots culturally acceptable, affordable and relevant primary health care systems;
- to disseminate knowledge of the health benefits of African medicinal plants;
- to carry out researches into ancient African healing systems with a view to modernizing them and making them available to the wider world through education;
- to demystify African traditional medicine and purge it of elements of occultism, fetishism and superstition, and promote its rational use to make it globally acceptable;
- to be a truly indigenous/exogenous herbal phyto-medicine centre that combines respect for nature and community with wealth creation.

Altogether, Dr Adodo now embraced worldviews, or realities, from all four corners of the globe. More specifically:

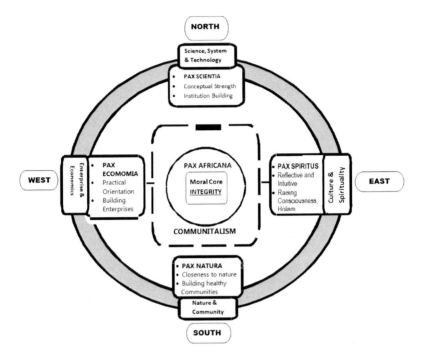

Figure 2.2 Pax Africana revisited.

Pax Natura: *south*: identified with Africa. Key features are: indigenous knowledge, community activation, agronomy, connection with the soil, respect and oneness with nature, a communversity of life. Orientation is towards NATURE and COMMUNALISM.

Pax Spritus: *east*: identified mainly with Asia. Key features are: emphasis on inner peace, wholeness, culture, inner security, spirituality, higher consciousness, intuition, feelings and emotions as part of human experience. Orientation is towards HOLISM.

Pax Scientia: *north*: identified mainly with Europe. Fully in control of advances in scientific theories and social theories. Key features are: political systems, institutionalized research, and control of the world's economic, political and social systems through colonization, capitalism, socialism, neo-liberalism, globalization, etc. Orientation is towards RATIONALISM.

Pax Economia: *west*: identified mainly with America. Known for business, enterprise, entrepreneurship, individual quest for profit and competition. Key features are: practical application of technology for profit, business management and dollarization of world economy. The orientation is towards PRAGMATISM.

Paxherbals: communitalism in action

At Paxherbals, Dr Father Anselm today and his 150 co-producers, supported by some 1,000 distributors around Nigeria, cultivate their own herbs directly and also through accredited local outgrowers. Paxherbals is the only herbal manufacturing company left in Nigeria that is locally producing its herbal medicines, despite the harsh economic climate which makes it easier and more profitable to be an importer rather than a manufacturer. It is no wonder that the Nigerian market is flooded with herbal products imported from foreign countries. By so doing, Nigeria is creating wealth abroad and promoting poverty at home.

Paxherbals believes that the only way to sustainable development is for Africa to produce what it consumes and consume what it produces. But to produce, one must innovate. Paxherbals is determined to continue to champion the preservation of African indigenous knowledge of African medicine, for the sake of posterity and for the sake of Pax Africana, an Africa Centre for Integral Research and Development (ACIRD).

Community activation, awakening consciousness, institutionalized research

The goal of ACIRD is to establish new templates for doing research *in* and *for* Africa. For centuries, Africans were a people spoken about, spoken for and spoken against by foreigners. We read about who we are from what others said and wrote about us. ACIRD seeks to assert the right of Africans to speak in their own language and metaphors. For Adodo, we must reclaim our right to cognitive freedom, if we truly seek to be free. Africa must be aware of, and fight against the coloniality of knowledge and *Epistemicide*, which are modern forms of colonization, by evolving and e-ducing (origin of the word education) its own research methods and research methodologies suited to and geared towards African epistemological emancipation.

Paxherbals, Pax Africana and ACIRD

ACIRD, a joint venture between Paxherbals locally, Ibadan University Centre for African Studies nationally, and Trans4m Center for Integral

Development globally, was constituted in May 2016, in fact soon after Father Anselm Adodo was awarded his PhD and PHD by Da Vinci Institute and Trans4m, respectively. Adodo is passionate about research, both processually and also substantively, that leads to social, if not also technological, innovation in Africa. African intellectuals in diverse fields do research for the sake of research: research that contributes little or nothing to the individual, and communal, organizational and societal development. We can now conclude.

Conclusion

How did Adodo develop from animateur to communal integrator?

Through the utilization of common plants and weeds, Paxherbal Clinic and Research Laboratories has been able to develop a natural science-based approach to developing herbal recipes that have been of help to the local community and to millions of Nigerians. It also has a home-grown economic model that puts the interests of the local community at its focal point. Rather than practise capitalist "free enterprise", which encourages the individual to acquire as much for himself as possible, Adodo has developed an economic model based on what he has termed *communitalism*.

Caring 4 integral development

Through community activation, followed by an awakening of an integral consciousness, leading to institutionalized research, Africa generally, according to Adodo, like Paxherbals specifically, must invest massively in knowledge. Such knowledge should serve to improve the social soil and environment on which it grows, keep abreast of knowledge development, set in motion dynamic knowledge-creating processes, reduce knowledge deficits, free knowledge from impurities, strengthen knowledge infrastructures and institutions, fight knowledge obsolescence and increase knowledge performance. Africans must embark on a new adventure of knowledge, moreover, ultimately involving institutionalized innovation driven research, leading to indigenous-exogenous knowledge-led sustainable development, harnessing nature power; fusing prayer (*ora*) and work (*labore*); combining nature, spirit, science and economy; culminating in organizational or societal communitalism, altogether centred in individual and community healing.

ACIRD then, through Paxherbals, the University of Ibadan Institute for African Studies and Trans4m, has taken up the challenge of filling part of the knowledge deficit prevalent in Africa, thereby turning from community activation and the awakening of African consciousness towards innovation-driven institutionalized research with a view to transformative education. The journey to a true Pax Africana has begun, now to be enriched by the origination of the path of reasoned realization, centred upon a so called *truth quest*, to which we now turn, for the grounding of the "north-western" research path.

References

Adodo, A. (2012) *Nature Power: A Christian Approach to Herbal Medicine.* Ewu-Esan, Nigeria: Benedictine Publications.

Adodo, A. (2016) *Communitalism.* PhD Thesis, Da Vinci Institute, South Africa.

Lessem, R. (2016) *The Integrators: Beyond Leadership, Knowledge and Value Creation.* Abingdon, UK: Routledge.

3 Truth quest

Grounding of the north-western path of reasoned realization

A primocracy perspective on community activation

Summary of chapter:

1   underpinned by direct democracy;
2   evolving through the evocation of a big restorative picture;
3   amplified by a discursive community;
4   effected via individual and group individuation;
5   serving to actualize a truth quest.

Introduction

Primal care

We now turn, by way of our "north western" *grounding* of community activation (see Figure 3.1), from the "southern" *relational* path of Chinyika (securing livelihoods) in Zimbabwe and the "eastern" path of renewal of Paxherbals (communal healing) in Nigeria, to the path of *reasoned realization,* centred in the *Truth Quest* pursued by South African born Louis

TENET 3 SG
Discursive Community (N/W)

TENET 4   *CORE TENET*   TENET 2 SG
Individuation (N/W) **Truth Quest (N/W)** *Big Picture (N/W)*
Herman/Agora/Greece

TENT 1 SG
Pursue Direct Democracy (N/W)

Figure 3.1 Reasoned community activation: grounded tenets.

Herman, a Professor of Political Science in Hawaii!, Herman himself being of "southern" African origins (see Table 3.1).

Overall then, what Herman is proposing is based especially on the San Bushmen and the Ancient Greek polis.

For us it is a kind of extrapolation, from a polity perspective, of what we have seen in Chinyika and around Paxherbals, in Southern and West Africa respectively, but has not yet been extended into politics writ large in Africa nationally. The question here is the extent to which you are building towards this, as summarized above as points of pre-emphasis on the reasoned path of realization, in your community activation.

In fact, Herman draws most specifically on both the ancient Greek polis and the Bushmen of Southern Africa for his consideration of a primal future (Herman, 2013). We have incorporated this into our integral polity, and here we allude to it as primocracy (Lessem et al., 2014). This serves to ground community activism in self-government in "north-western" guise.

Democratic community to the searching growing individual

Our modern use of the word *politics*, whether in Zimbabwe or America, Nigeria or Slovenia, has been thoroughly debased and misunderstood as in practice it is commonly used, according to Herman, to describe ways and means of seeking and wielding power over others for personal gain. On the scale of public opinion, he says, politicians rank somewhere "between prostitutes and used-car-salesmen". The whole business of politics is

Table 3.1 Grounded CARE for primocracy

Grounding communal activation: truth quest north-western path of reasoned realization healthy participatory co-existence via self-government
• *Communal attributes*: grounding – livelihood, healing, truth quest; emergence – permaculture, healing, new worlds; navigation – networks, study circles, participatory; effect – community building, self-sufficiency, mutual aid.
• *Integrator role*: community steward, e.g. *Louis Herman*.
• *Communal function*: truth quest followed in a community.
• *Grounded in value*: the build up of *local value* provides the ground for *direct democracy*; enhances the culture through sharing the *restorative big picture*; provides a *communally discursive* means of navigation; providing the *common sense of ownership* underlying it; characterized by a powerful contribution to *group individuation*; altogether at a community's best resulting in; at worst the big man syndrome prevails.

considered as far from its European Socratic roots in philosophy and "cultivating virtue" as one can get.

To move out of this dead end, he maintains, we need to retrace our steps to find a way forward. If we go back two and a half thousand years to Ancient Greece, we can find the origin of the word politics in the Greek *polis* – the self-governing, autonomous, democratic city state – where politics simply referred to the affairs of the polis. As the concern of all, it was regarded as the most enobling and meaningful of all human activities. However, Herman then reaches even further back to the San Bushmen of Southern Africa. Hence he draws on both ancient African and European roots for his primocracy.

Herman then uses the word politics in the original, inclusive sense, to mean the universal human struggle, individually and collectively, to seek and to live the best possible life. Political philosophy can then be reconnected to its original Socratic intention as the search for the "the good life". Primocracy, for you, then presents a model of what Herman calls "the truth quest" – and we term a *shared truth quest* – as an archetypal dynamic of the human search for order, as for example in the Chinyika and Paxherbals cases we have already seen, which itself becomes the core of a new political practice. The model, as we interpret it, is comprised of four interconnected elements, these being:

- participation in a *democratic community* (our "south");
- construction of a *restorative big picture* of our shared reality (our "east");
- honest face-to-face *communal discussion* (our "north"); and the
- understanding of *group individuation* (our "west").

What does this mean altogether for your pursuit of community activation?

The mandala-integral structure

The mandala of primal politics

The mandala structure below (Figure 3.2), for Herman, functions like a Jungian archetype, drawn from the Swiss psychoanalyst, Carl Jung, a deeply rooted way of thinking and behaving. The four quadrants of the mandala represent the distinctiveness of each element. The surrounding circle represents their interconnectedness in continual dynamic interaction, converging in the unity of the single centrepoint – the quest itself.

Since the mandala of primal politics is rooted in the deep structure of what it means to be human, it can function effectively, in Herman's view, as an ideal offering global criteria for development, without necessarily having to

NAVIGATION
Face-to-Face
Socratic Discussion

Shamanism
The Whole Person   Religion   The Big Picture
Individuation   TRUTH QUEST – *CENTRE* Big Story/ Myth
EFFECT   Philosophy   *EMERGENCE*
Science

The Whole
Community/Direct Democracy
GROUNDING

Figure 3.2 The mandala of primocracy.

be embodied in small-scale self-sufficient local communities, such as that of Chinyika or indeed Paxherbals in Edo State, as we have seen in the previous two chapters. Its values can guide us in whatever institutional, national or historical setting we find ourselves towards actualization of the optimum form of polity. The more completely we together understand the big story, the better able we are to respond creatively to the challenges of our moment by applying the discipline of the mandala. We now deal with each of the four elements in turn, which underlie in your case community activation.

With respect to each one, you may ask yourself to what extent are you engaged with each: whole community, shared big picture, face-to-face communal discussion, and overall process of group individuation, altogether underlined by your particular truth quest, or what we term inner – aligned with outer – calling?

Engage with the whole community

Direct democracy, first, expresses the value of communication free from the distortions of concentrated wealth and power. It also expresses a society's commitment to providing the education and resources necessary to maximize the individual's participation in face-to-face decision-making.

Nelson Mandela (Mandela, 1994), for example, gives us a vivid description of such direct communal democracy from his youth, when he lived with the Regent at Mqhekezweni, the seat of the tribal chiefdom of his Thembu people. For him:

Everyone who wanted to speak did so. It was democracy in its purest form. There may have been a hierarchy of importance amongst the speakers, but everyone was heard, chief and subject, warrior and medicine man, shopkeeper and farmer.

We also see something approximating to direct democracy in the early days of the Israeli kibbutz (Russell *et al.*, 2014), for example, when all adult members of the community gathered in the general assembly to make collective decisions for the community through face-to-face discussion. The San Bushmen give us our most complete model of direct democracy where each individual participates directly in decision-making. Each also relates directly to the entire non-human community of being – surrounding wilderness – as an integral part of political reality. Each is free to come and go as he or she pleases. As is typical among many hunting-gathering societies, the San have no powerful chiefs. As one individual remarked to a visiting anthropologist inquiring about chiefs in this much vaunted egalitarian society: "Of course we have chiefs! Each one of us is a chief over himself". The same ultimately applied to the Women's Council in Chinyika.

We now turn to the "big picture".

The restorative big picture

Big pictures are symbolic representations of the whole. They are visions paradigms, worldviews and epic narratives that serve to connect the lives and passions of the individual to larger, more encompassing realities – family, tribe, nation, civilization, species and ultimately the living earth and the evolving cosmos. Such a restorative picture is conveyed by the poem recited at Chinyika to celebrate the revival of rapoko or finger millet in the community:

> The grass that pervades through every aspect of the Chinyika people's lives
> The grass that makes delicious food and drinks
> The grass that is used to celebrate success and to talk to the ancestral spirits
> The grass that gives the human body everything it needs.
> The grass that makes and gives life to people, the grass that turns to gold the magical grass.

Without such nested pictures of wholes within wholes, or stories within stories, we drift, unprepared, easily surprised and distracted. Our energies become dissipated, and we lapse into selfishness and cynicism. These big pictures only become politically significant and morally compelling to the degree that they are processed through the mill of the other mandala components – self-reflecting individuals, similarly motivated, in free discussion within the community. Today, according to Herman, we are in crisis because we are in between cosmologies. We have no consensus about a story of origin and meaning that expresses the reality of the contemporary human condition.

Herman offers the mandala dynamic as the core organizing feature of a new story. It is unlike any previous story in its reflexivity; it recognizes the gradual emergence of storytelling in a community of individuating individuals as the defining feature of a future primal politics, accompanying communal activation. He shows how this dynamic emerged in small-scale, self-sufficient, self-organizing communities, like Chinyika, still living close to nature. He then describes it reappearing in history in times of social upheaval and transformation.

Face-to-face communal discussion

Face-to-face communal discussion confronts our personal truths with that of a diversity of communal others, each on his or her own trajectory through life. Such communication offers a direct way for grasping the dialectical logic of truth through contradiction, since it confronts us in the most inescapable way possible with our in between situation. We are constituted by a larger shared communal reality, which each individual experiences differently. Honest, empathic engagement of the other is essential to grasping a larger whole. Individuation promotes coming to consensus through discussion and discussion stimulates individuation, of individual and group. It is significant that the Greek polis that gave us philosophy and direct democracy grounded both in face-to-face discussion.

The face-to-face situation is at its most universal in the primal band. Bushman politics, for example, swam in an ocean of discussion and storytelling. The same applied to co-creators, Muchineripi and Kada, in Zimbabwe. In such situations, the individual is stimulated and challenged to keep thinking and move around the medicine wheel of life – to keep growing as an individual.

Engage in group individuation

Finally, for Herman, all our knowing is inevitably refracted through our unique trajectory through life, for self and others, such as that of Muchineripi's/Chinyika's story or Father Anselm's/Paxherbals (see Chapters 1 and 2). As we struggle to grasp a shared reality, we are forced to reflect on our uniqueness and to recognize that of others, together.

Certain socio-economic structures enhance this process; others repress it. The small size and self-sufficiency of the primal hunting group impelled every adult to participate in all the definitively human activities: hunter, gatherer, artist, healer, musician, learner and teacher. Conversely, the social hierarchy and division of labour of classical and industrial societies restricts the degree to which the individual can play multiple parts in the life of the community. The Greek ideal of *arête* or excellence was the cultivation of the whole person, the consummate amateur who would participate creatively in all aspects of life and thus grasp the fullest range of what it meant to be human, set within the context of the Greek polis. The African notion of *ubuntu* – "I am because you are" – is another case in point.

In fact, Nelson Mandela's capacity, in the course of his 27-year internment, to discover and affirm within his own soul the Afrikaner oppressor transformed both himself and his jailers. His example made it possible for a majority of South Africans, poised on the edge of a racial war, to envision a multiracial polity, or "rainbow nation" and a nonviolent reconciliation after apartheid. The good life requires this paradoxical individuality, on the one hand free and self-directed, and on the other, connected in a loving relationship to the entire community of beings.

Conclusion: in pursuit of a truth quest

When, according to Herman, we look at what the great revolutionary paradigm builders of western civilization actually did, as opposed to what they told us we should do, we can see some patterns roughly equivalent to the practices constituting the truth quest described in what we term primocracy. Socrates and Plato, Machiavelli, Hobbes, Locke, Rousseau and Marx were passionately involved in the troubles of their times, all in pursuit of a truth quest.

They all responded out of a heightened awareness of the human predicament of living in the in between (individual and collective), as has been the case for Muchineripi and Kada, and for Father Anselm Adodo, here for Louis Herman and potentially now in your own community activation case. The mandala, for Herman, like our own integral worlds, offers a model for communal activation leading to political and economic transformation without overt power plays, since it works continually to challenge the lure of power and privilege with love for the beauty of the path with a heart. It involves the build up of a direct democracy, the crafting of a restorative big picture, the development of a discursive community, and ultimately group individuation, resulting overall in pursuit of a truth quest. To what extent then does this apply in your own case?

We now turn from our local grounding of community activation, primarily in Africa, to local-global emergence of such community activation in developing and developed worlds, starting out with the pursuit of *natural value*. As we move for each path from grounding to emergence, so the key tenets of such move to the background rather than occupying the foreground, though they still provide an important perspective. We now turn to *permaculture* and the emergent trajectory of the renewal path extending community activation, by aligning it with an initial awakening of integral consciousness, while retaining our emphasis on community activation, thereby Care-ing.

References

Herman, L. (2013) *Future Primal: How Our Wilderness Origins Show Us the Way Forward.* Novato, CA: New World Library.

Lessem, R., Abouleish, I., Pogacnik, M. and Herman, L. (2014) *Integral Polity.* Abingdon, UK: Routledge.

Mandela, N. (1994) *The Long Walk to Freedom.* New York: Ballantyne.

Russell, R., Hanneman, R. and Getz, S. (2013) *The Renewal of the Kibbutz: Competing Constructions in Modern Culture.* New Brunswick, NJ: Rutgers University Press.

Part II

Eastern emergence of community

Permaculture, vitality of place, disclose
new worlds

4   Permaculture

Emergence via awakening of the relational path

An ecodynamic perspective on community activation

Summary of chapter:

1   pursuing Earth justice following "wild" as opposed to "natural" law;
2   integrally healing the Earth through eco-economic exchange;
3   building cultural, social and economic worth organizationally/societally;
4   participating communally or organizationally in the great work of nature;
5   altogether centred in permaculture as an interdisciplinary Earth science.

Introduction: emergence of community activation via relational path

CAre for community-in-nature

Up to now our focus has been on "southern" grounding of community activation, on the relational, renewal, and reasoned realization paths respectively, serving to secure livelihoods, heal communities and pursuing a truth quest, primarily in and around Africa. We now turn locally-globally to such community activation that has emerged above and beyond a particular locale, spreading from south and east to north and west. We also adopt a more dynamic, *emergent perspective* at a higher level of abstraction – eco/dynamic, developmental, renewal oriented – than has been so before, thereby beginning to awaken integral consciousness (Figure 4.1).

Permaculture as integral awakening of community activation

Bill Mollison, an Australian jack-of-all-trades, together with his compatriot and ecologist, David Holmgren (Holmgren, 2002), after extensive research

TENETS LG3/LE 3
Build Up Social Capital
Cultural, Political and Economic Commonwealth

TENETS LG 4/LE 4	CORE TENET LG/LE	TENETS LG 2/LE 2
Community Ownership	*Community*	*Add Natural Value*
Great Work of Nature	*Activation/*	Integrally Heal the Earth
	Secure Livelihood	
	Permaculture	
	Mollison/Shiva/Berry	

TENETS LG1/LE 1
Underlying Ubuntu
Pursue Earth Justice

Figure 4.1 Relational community activation: key emergent tenets.

into the Tasmanian aborigines, evolved and first publicized in the 1970s what they termed *permaculture*: permanent agriculture (Table 4.1). They deemed it, in now integral relational guise, an "interdisciplinary earth science with a potential for a positive, integrated, and global outreach". The agricultural system that they developed incorporated a comprehensive paradigm shift that involved the development of an ethical and moral (relational) and developmental (integral) approach to the natural world.

The foundation of this ethic began with the adoption of a "sophisticated aboriginal belief system":

> Life (according to the aboriginal people of Australia) is a totality neither created nor destroyed. It can be imagined as an egg from which all tribes (life forms) issue and to which all return. The ideal way in which to spend one's time is in the perfection of the expression of life, to lead the most evolved life possible, and to assist in and celebrate the existence of life forms other than humans, for all come from the same egg.
>
> (Sveiby and Skuthorpe, 2006)

Community activation, in this guise, is close to nature.

The wisdom of the world's oldest Nhungabarra people

Indeed, from a natural and cultural perspective, for the aboriginal Nhungabarra people, for fellow indigenous Australian Tex Skuthorpe

Table 4.1 Emergent CARE: permaculture

Emergent communal activation: permaculture *emergent southern relational path the integral contribution of permaculture*
• *Communal attributes*: grounding – livelihood, healing, truth quest; emergence – *permaculture*, vitality of place, disclosing new worlds; navigation – participatory, study circles, networks; effect – community building, self-sufficiency, mutual advantage. • *Integrator role*: community steward, e.g. *Bill Mollison, Vandana Shiva.* • *Communal function*: communal learning and development through which communities' *nature and culture co-evolve*. • *Grounded in value*: value arises out of a sense of *Earth justice* providing a sense of purpose; builds on culture and nature thereby *integrally healing the Earth*; is sourced through *cultural, political and economic threefolding* in a community; ultimately we respect creation whereby such communities *contribute to the great work of nature*; at their worst rigid localism prevails.

and exogenous Sweden's knowledge management consultant Karl Sveiby (Sveiby and Skuthorpe, 2006), the stories and their hidden meanings constitute their archives, law book, educational text book, country maps and Bible. These in fact convey four levels of meaning. Its first level is the text itself and its explained *natural features* and *animal behaviours*. The natural environment thus reinforces learning on a daily basis. Typically, this first level is also exciting and entertaining.

The second level of meaning concerns the *relationships between the people in the community*. There are an infinite number of truths and *what is true for one person is not true for another*. The third level concerns the *relationship between your own community and the wider environment*. That is the earth and the other Aboriginal communities. You have to pull out the meaning yourself, and you need to have some knowledge of the law as such. Many, but not all stories, have a fourth level. This ultimate level taught *spiritual action and psychic skills*; it was more doing than talking and listening. This fourth level included *practice, ceremonies and experiences*, which gave access to special esoteric knowledge hidden in the story. The notion of the "aboriginal", in fact, might be aligned with that of the "wild" and for this we turn from Australasia to Southern Africa.

A Southern African manifesto for Earth justice

For South African environmental lawyer Cormac Cullinan (Cullinan, 2004), it is precisely the false dichotomy between the "wild" and the "law", between "nature" and "civilization", that we, in relation to nature and community, seek to overcome. Like the Chinese symbol for Yin and Yang, both wildness and lawfulness are part of a whole, and it is the dynamic balance between them that is important, not the triumph of one over the other. In fact, to stamp out wildness and promote the dull conformity of monoculture, for Cullinan, is not desirable. To what extent then do you incorporate such "wildness" in activating your community or communities?

Much of what is best in us, Cullinan says, is contained within our "wild" hearts. Wildness is associated with creativity and passion, with that part of us which is most connected with nature. It can also be understood as a metaphor for the life force, or indeed *vital force* that flows through us all and drives the evolutionary process. In this sense, it has an eternal, scared quality that both defines us and connects us most intimately with this planet. Wildness is a quality that can only be experienced by straying off the orthodox path of civilization as we know it.

We now turn from "south" towards the "east", still retaining our concern for the activation of *nature* and community, but now also informed by culture and consciousness, thereby further heightening our integral awareness.

Emerging in the east: vitality of the sun – designed to last

Tapping into the natural vitality of the sun

Ibrahim Abouleish (Abouleish, 2005) was born and bred in Egypt and pursued his doctoral studies in Austria, before taking up a senior research post at a pharmaceutical laboratory there. In his early forties, though, he felt the urge to return to his homeland, to make a contribution to his country in need. "The Prophet says every one of you is a shepherd, and everyone is responsible for those under your protection". After he had positioned the first roads and plotted the fields, in the desert plot he purchased adjacent to Cairo, the next task was to drill two wells. He did not know how to do this so he was lucky to have to employ people to terrace the ground and dig canals for the water to flow to the fields.

Thereby they ultimately co-created Sekem, a marriage of occident and orient. During his initial years in Austria, Abouleish, on the way to such, had absorbed much of European culture, particularly that of Rudolf Steiner's anthroposophy, and the biodynamic farming methods derived from it. Through this cross-cultural exchange, he could perceive his own roots, specifically in Islam, from a totally different perspective. This kindled the first flame of his vision. After much consideration he chose the name Sekem for it; the reason being that "the Egyptians had recognised the light and warmth of the sun as well as the third life giving force, vitality, permeating and enlivening the earth's entire being".

The economic life of Sekem, as such, begins at a practical level to "heal" the earth through biodynamic methods. In partnership with close friends and colleagues in Europe, and local partners in trade, Sekem marketed their products through what they termed "the economics of love". Its cultural life evolved, whereby the ultimately integral enterprise pursued research into all walks of life, educating children, youth and adults in cognitive and practical skills, while enhancing their free will, and, of late, prospectively creating a university for sustainable development, spanning agriculture and health, engineering and economics.

We now turn from the middle to the further east, to the Philippines in fact, for Perlas' approach to "threefolding".

Shaping globalization: civil society, cultural power, threefolding

Nicanor Perlas (Perlas, 2000) is a leading social activist at the Centre for Alternative Development Initiatives in the Philippines. *Threefolding*, for him, as for Ibrahim Abouleish above, drawing on the original insights of Austrian social philosopher Rudolph Steiner, brings an integral and holistic approach to the process and substance of development and can either increase or harmonize the conflict between the three global forces – cultural, political and economic – that inhabit the tri-polar world. With the coming of the new millennium, humanity faces a great and unique challenge. The right kind of global economic integration now makes it possible for humanity to create a planetary understanding of culture, love, respect and cooperation. Alternatively, globalization can give certain elite segments of society the power to impose a living hell on earth. As beings endowed with creative spiritual powers, humanity faces a fateful moment in its long evolutionary journey. Will we shape freedom to win freedom, peace and prosperity, as Maathai has also intimated, and as "Agenda 21" has advocated? Or will we mould globalization to be an engine of planetary destruction?

For Perlas, the specific origins of *Philippine Agenda 21* (PA21) can be traced back to 1992, when newly elected Philippine President Fidel Ramos invited 18 civil society leaders for a dialogue on sustainable development. In PA21 the Philippines articulated an image of society that is threefold, that is culture, polity and economy, altogether engaged with nature and community. It also identified the three key actors of society as civil society in the realm of culture, government in the realm of polity, and business with labour in the realm of economy.

To further our trans-cultural and trans-disciplinary dynamic evolution of community activation, we turn now from the "east" to the European "north", thereby spanning southern, eastern, northern and western Europe.

Navigating from the north: living within the truth

Beyond capitalism and socialism: grounded in the natural world

Vaclav Havel (Havel, 1989), the first President of the Czech Republic, was unique in being a European Head of State who was also a playwright and a social philosopher, having been a noted dissident under the former communist regime. Living within the truth for Havel is an elementary starting point for every attempt made by people to oppose the alienating pressure of the system. If it is the only meaningful basis of any independent act of political import, and if, ultimately, it is also the most intrinsically existential source of the dissident's attitude, then it is difficult to imagine that even manifest dissidence could have any other basis than the service of truth, the truthful life and the attempt to make room for the genuine aims of life.

Above all, any existential revolution should provide hope of a moral reconstitution of society, which means a radical renewal of the relationship of human beings to what Havel calls the human order, which no political order can replace. Thereby a new experience of being, a renewed rootedness in the universe, a newly grasped sense of higher responsibility, a new-found inner relationship to other people and to the human community, including nature and agriculture, these factors clearly indicate the direction in which we must go. For centuries, the basic component of European agriculture had been the family farm. In Czech, the older term for it was "grunt". The word, taken from the German "grund", actually means ground or foundation. The colloquial synonym in Czech actually means ground or foundation, or indeed groundedness. What then is the equivalent in your society?

We now turn from the Czech Republic to its northern European neighbour, Austria, and from the statesman and playwright, Havel, to the physicist and ecologist, Capra, and thereby from the humanities to the sciences, from the natural "grund" to living networks. In fact, as we turn from "south" and "east" to "north" we can see how the university world comes more into play.

Autopoeisis: a science for sustainable living

Sustained life, for Austro-American physicist and ecologist Fritjof Capra (Capra, 2002), is a property of an ecological system rather than a single organism of species. Traditional biology has tended to concentrate attention on individual organisms rather than on the biological continuum. The origin of life is thus looked for as a unique event in which an organism arises from the surrounding milieu. A more ecologically balanced point of view, for Capra, would examine the proto-ecological cycles and subsequent chemical systems that must have developed and flourished while objects resembling organisms appeared.

According to the Gaia theory of British geophysicist James Lovelock and American biologist Lyn Marguilis, "the evolution of the first living organisms went hand in hand with the transformation of the planetary surface from an inorganic environment to a self-regulating biosphere" (Capra, 2002). In that sense, life is a property of planets rather than of individual organisms. As ecosystems are understood in terms of food webs (networks of organisms) so organisms are viewed by Capra as networks of cells, organs and organ systems, and cells as networks of molecules.

"Wherever we see life, we see networks. This is the key to the systemic definition of life: living networks continually create, or recreate, themselves by transforming or replacing their components" (Capra, 2002). In this way, they undergo continual structural changes while preserving their web-like patterns of organization. This dynamic of self-generation is seen as a key characteristic of life by biologists, Chile's Humberto Maturana and France's Francisco Varela, who gave it the name *autopoeisis*, literally "self making".

We now turn from the scientifically based Europe, generally, to the more experimentally based America, more specifically.

Western natural effect: respecting creation to natural work

Respecting creation

Native Indian, or "First Nation", indigenous intellectual traditions, for American Indian theologian George Tinker (Tinker, 2008), conceive of the world as a constant creative process that requires our continual participation. Respect for "creation" emerges out of our perceived need for maintaining balance in the world around us. When the balance of existence is disturbed, whole communities pay a price. The notion of reciprocity, moreover, is fundamental to such balance and harmony. Wherein does such lie in your case?

As a most fundamental creation symbol, moreover, the significance of the circle is its genuine egalitarian-ness. There is no way to make it hierarchical. The cross within the circle symbolizes the four directions, and the four two-legged nations that walk the earth: Black, Yellow, White and Red. It also signifies the two-legged, four-legged, winged, and living-moving creatures.

We now turn from Native America to the American Kentucky heartlands, continuing on from where the First Peoples leave off.

The great natural work

For Kentucky-based farmer and nature lover, Wendell Berry (Berry, 1999), the *Great Work of the First Peoples*, as we have seen, was to establish an intimate relationship with earth powers through such ceremonies as the Great Thanksgiving of the Iroquois, and the vision quest of Plains Indians. In North America, though, it is with a poignant feeling of foreboding concerning the future that Berry acknowledges that "the European occupation of the continent, however admirable its intentions, has been flawed from the beginning in its assault on the indigenous peoples and its plundering of the land".

If there was also advancement of scientific insight and technological skills leading to relief from many of the ills and poverty of the European peoples, this advancement was accompanied by the devastation of this continent in its natural fluorescence, by the suppression of the way of life of its indigenous peoples and by communicating to them many previously unknown diseases. "The Great Work now", as we move into a new millennium, Berry says, "is to carry out the transition from a period of human devastation of the earth to a period when humans would be present to the planet in a mutually beneficial manner". What then does that mean for you, in the context of such community activation and natural restoration?

The earth, as such, would be our primary teacher in industry and economics, teaching us how to minimize entropy. A healing of the earth, for Berry, is a prerequisite for the healing of the human. In conclusion we return, overall, to community economic development, at least from the view point of a prominent Canadian community activist.

Conclusion: community economic development

Self-reliance to community culture

We have now completed the integral *dynamic* journey from grounding to effect, from south to east onto north and then west. For Marcia Nozick (Nozick, 1993), a Canadian community activist, the most critical issue we face, together with environmental destruction, is the disappearance of community, both on a physical and a spiritual level. As a result, communities are breaking apart under the strain of outward-pulling forces of global economic development.

There are, then, for Novick, five major principles or action areas which, taken together, provide a framework for building sustainable communities, or for us underlying community activation. They are gaining *economic self-reliance*; becoming *ecologically sustainable*; attaining *community control*: empowering community members to make decisions affecting their community, workplace and lives; *meeting the basic needs* of individuals; *building a community culture* – to know who we are. Which of these most apply in your case?

Community activation aligned with integral consciousness

What then does this all mean for us, as a global community, in terms of development studies as a whole? How might community activation on the local ground further evolved locally-globally, now result in a newly global approach to development that builds on what has come locally and locally-globally before?

Overall then, via an emergent relational path, the pursuit of earth justice; integrally healing the earth; the build up of cultural, socio-political and economic commonwealth; and participation in the great work of nature, culminates in permaculture.

We now turn from emergent community activation *eco-dynamics* (Lessem, 2013), specifically co-evolving such permaculture, to integral *development*, specifically turning to *vitality of place*.

References

Abouleish, A. (2005) *Sekem – A Sustainable Community in the Desert.* Edinburgh, UK: Floris.

Berry, T. (1999) *The Great Work: Our Way into the Future.* New York: Bell Tower.

Capra, F. (2002) *The Hidden Connections – A Science For Sustainable Living.* New York: HarperCollins.

Cullinan, C. (2004) *Wild Law: Manifesto for Earth Justice.* Totnes, UK: Green Books.

Havel, V. (1989) *Living in Truth.* London: Faber and Faber.

Holmgren, D. (2002) *Permaculture: Principles and Pathways beyond Sustainability.* Victoria, Australia: Holmgren Design Services.

Lessem, R., Schieffer, A., Rima, S. and Tong, J. (2013) *Integral Dynamics: Cultural Dynamics, Political Economy and Business Administration.* Abingdon, UK: Routledge.

Nozick, M. (1993) 'Five principles of sustainable community development'. In Shragge, E. (ed.) *Community Economic Development: In Search of Empowerment.* Montreal, Canada: Black Rose Books.

Perlas, N. (2000) *Shaping Globalisation.* Cape Town, South Africa: Novalis.

Sveiby, K. and Skuthorpe, T. (2006) *Treading Lightly: The Hidden Wisdom of the World's Oldest People.* London: Allen and Unwin.

Tinker, G. (2008) *American Indian Liberation – A Theology of Sovereignty.* New York. Orbis Books.

5   Vitality of place

Emergence via awakening of the path of renewal

A developmental perspective on community activation

Summary of chapter:

1   underpinned by an underlying socio-economic value base;
2   enhanced by communal relationships, within your organization or without;
3   your community and/or enterprise are socially embedded institutions;
4   resulting in trade and accumulation both micro and macro in nature;
5   culminating in the vitality of a particular place.

Introduction: development studies and the vitality of place

Embedding CARE

We now turn from eco-dynamic to developmental CARE, with a specific focus on community activation from an overall developmental – and thereby more integral – perspective, on now the emergent foundation of the path of renewal (Figure 5.1). We thereby turn from the local, to the local-global. This, if you like, is the Chinyika or Paxherbals story writ large, something generally absent from the development studies agenda. *Vitality of place* therefore is set within the context of our approach to integral – self, organizational, communal and societal – development (Schieffer and Lessem, 2014).

In fact, most developmental thinking, societally speaking, has taken place in a rather distant, intellectualized manner. As a result, much of the subsequent work has thereby proven to be out of touch with the actually experienced life worlds and cultural contexts of the people, such as those at Chinyika and Edo State (see Chapters 1 and 2) that it seeks to benefit. The reason for this is that such a societal approach has not emerged out of

TENETS NG3/NE 3
Combining Nature, Spirit, Science, Economy
Integrally Embedded Institutions

TENETS NG 4/NE 4	CORE TENET LG/LE	TENETS NG 2/NE 2
Communitalism	*Community*	*Fusing Work and Prayer*
Trade and Accumulation	*Activation/*	Communal Relationships
	Heal Community	
	Vitality of Place	
	Escobar/Gudeman	

TENETS NG1/NE 1
Nature Power
Socio-economic Value Base

Figure 5.1 Renewed community activation: key emergent tenets.

these very individual and communal contexts, in Zimbabwe, in Nigeria, and so on. As a result, it is plucked out of societal mid air, usually from developmental thinkers based in the US or Europe. Among such there is only a relatively small group of primarily anthropologists that have not only delved into the depth of such contexts, but also managed to understand local conditions and see development with the communal eyes of those "to be activated or developed". Most of such work is based in South America, involving anthropologists who straddle the North-South American divide.

The nature of community

The natural collective starting point for working with society then, as we have seen, is the immediate community, on the ground. Starting there, rather than with society as a whole, helps us to bring things back to human scale, back into a sphere where interaction is possible and tangible. UK-based social activist Geoff Mulgan (Mulgan, 2005), founder of the British think tank Demos, for example, has a similar reason to ours as to why he prefers community as a starting point.

> Community is deliberately a different word from society. It may refer to neighbourhoods or workplaces, but to be meaningful it must imply membership in a human-scale collective: a scale at which it is possible to encounter people face to face . . . and to nurture human-scale

structures within which people can feel at home. Social science is ill at ease with such ideas. Strangely there is very little theory about the importance of scale and form in economics and sociology.

Development as a whole life project

An emergent process rooted in communal grounds

For anthropologist Arturo Escobar (Escobar, 2008), a renowned Colombian American voice (now based as an academic at Duke University in the US) in the development arena, such development studies have predominantly fostered a way of conceiving of social life as a technical problem, as a matter of rational decision and management to be entrusted to "specialized" development professionals. Usually "economic" knowledge qualified them for the task. Escobar argues that:

> [i]nstead of seeing development as an emergent process rooted in the grounds of each society's history, cultural tradition, human psyche, and existing indigenous institutions, these development professionals sought to devise mechanisms and procedures to make society fit a pre-existing imported economic model that embodied the structures and functions of modernity.

Development assumed a teleology that proposed that the original "natives" will sooner or later be reformed from without, rather than developmentally from within. In other words, the indigenous self and organization are either bypassed, or else accommodated in their traditionally static form, rather than enabled to re-form, thereby combining tradition with modernity. At the same time, it reproduced endlessly the separation between reformers and those to be reformed by keeping alive the image of the *underdeveloped* Third World. This world was deemed different and inferior, having limited "civilization" in relation to the accomplished, "developed" First World, and needing to be modernized.

Rethinking development at two levels

There are then two levels that must be considered in rethinking development from a nature and communal perspective. The first refers to the need to make explicit the existence of a plurality of models of the community-and-economy. This requires the development agent to place him or herself in the space of local "grounds". But this by itself will not make it. A second concern must be added. One – including those involved in communal activation – must have a theory about the forces underlying such. Escobar's claim that development needs to be seen as a whole life, or for us whole community, project, rather than merely focusing on its economic aspects, is strongly supported by the Hungarian intellectual Karl Polanyi, who was one of the first voices who warned of the negative consequences of an economy that dominates society, rather than being embedded in it.

Embedding livelihood and economics in society

Substantive and formal communities and economies

The Anglo-Hungarian economic anthropologist Karl Polanyi (Polanyi, 2001) was one of the great development economists in the first half of the twentieth century. Albeit that his work has been largely ignored by the economic establishment, it has been recognized in development thinking, as Björn Hettne (Hettne, 2009) stresses in his book on *Thinking about Development*. The reason why Polanyi's work has been bypassed by economists was that his approach was substantively anthropological, working upwards from the local community.

For Polanyi, in referring to human activities, the term economic is a compound of two meanings that have independent roots. Polanyi calls them substantive and formal. The substantive meaning of economics ("oikos" – ancient Greek for household, house or family) derives from man's dependence for his living on nature and his fellows. It refers to the interchange with his natural and social environment, insofar as this results in supplying him with the means of material want–satisfaction. How then does this arise in your case? The anthropologist, the sociologist and the historian then, each in his study of the place occupied by the economy in human society, is therefore faced, Polanyi emphasizes, with a great variety of institutions other than markets, in which man's livelihood is embedded.

The formal meaning of economics, Polanyi laments, is derived from abstract mathematical formulae, devoid of any natural, community-oriented, psychological or spiritual connotations. Concentrating on numerically derived demand and supply curves, mediated by price-based equilibria, is the formal economic approach par excellence. Here, economic activities are determined by choices induced by an insufficiency of means. The conceptual tools by which this is performed make up the discipline of economic analysis. The use of this formal meaning denotes the economy as a sequence of acts of economizing, that is of choices induced by scarcity situations.

Economy embedded in community and society

In conclusion, Polanyi argued not only for a perspective on development that put the economy in the midst rather than on top, of society. The economy is to be embedded, integrally for us, in society and seen in its interdependent relationship with society and a wide range of supporting and contributing institutions from all sectors of society. In the 1940s, he had indicated in his famous *The Great Transformation*, the deficiency of conventional economic development models and "the need to ground any approach to economic development firmly in the particular societal hand". Stephen Gudeman, to whom we now turn, does exactly that.

Unleashing community potential

There is no one true model of economy

Stephen Gudeman (Gudeman, 2001), uniquely both a graduate of Cambridge University's School of Anthropology in the UK and also Harvard Business School in the US, is today a professor emeritus in the department of anthropology at the University of Minnesota. For Gudeman, there is no one "true" model of economy, but only multiple meaningful formulations within particular cultures, each with their own value domains, in which we need to reflectively immerse ourselves as researchers (Table 5.1). Thereby we uncover the origins of a particular community. As a representative of modern economic anthropology, a school of thought that uses anthropology in trying to understand economy in human terms, he calls on us to understand "local models".

Table 5.1 Vital CARE.

Communal activation: vitality of place emergent *path of renewal contributes to* *emergent vitality*
• *Communal attributes*: grounding – livelihood, healing, truth quest; emergence – permaculture, *vitality of place*, disclosing new worlds; navigation – participatory, study circles, networks; effect – community building, self-sufficiency, mutual advantage. • *Integrator role*: community steward e.g. *Escobar, Gudeman*. • *Communal function*: communal learning and development through which communities are lodged in the *vitality of place*. • *Grounded in value*: *value* provides the *base* and the purpose; is sourced through *communal relationships*; builds on the culture through *trade* and *accumulation*; at best such *integrally embedded institutions* make a powerful contribution to society; at their worst parochialism, corruption and nepotism prevails.

Community and market

For Gudeman, economy consists of two realms, which he calls community and market. Both facets make up economy, for humans are motivated by social fulfilment, curiosity, and the pleasure of mastery, as well as by instrumental purpose, competition and the accumulation of gains. In one guise (community), economy is local and specific, constituted through social relationships and contextually defined values. In the other guise (market), it is impersonal, even global, and abstracted from social context.

Local value domains

In addition to community and market as the two constituting realms for economic practices and relationships, Gudeman distinguishes four value domains: base, relationships, trade and accumulation, the first two of which, for us – how might this be the case for you – are closely linked to community activation.

The first value domain then is the base or foundation. It consists of a community of shared interests, which include lasting resources, such as land and water, produced things and ideational constructs such as knowledge, technology, laws, practices, skills and customs. The base comprises cultural agreements and beliefs that provide a structure for all other domains.

The second domain, relationships, consists of valued communal connections maintained as ends in themselves. Through these relationships the base is created, allotted and apportioned to people in community.

The third and fourth domains consist of trade and accumulation. Accumulated value includes resources, relationships, goods, money and capital, all of which may become components of other domains. Amassed value is held, invested, consumed and displayed. Such an overall perspective of a social and economic base and its accompanying value domains, has, for us, distinct "southern" connotations, not surprisingly, given Gudeman's anthropological background.

Innovation in communal relationships

For Gudeman, "development is not primarily about capital accumulation, but rather about innovation in the relationships of you, your immediate community, your external community, organisations and society". Community in this wider sense offers, for him, a reservoir of possibilities, and the key to development is to unleash the innovative potential that lies in it. One important dimension for such unleashing lies in what Arturo Escobar calls the *vitality of place*.

Conclusion

The approach to economic and societal development that economic anthropologists like Stephen Gudeman, Arturo Escobar and Karl Polanyi have adopted, has also aligned the vitality of place, and for us community activation, with economy and society. For them, grounding in physical as well as human nature precedes the emergence of "embedded institutions", from which new community-based forms of economic behaviour are derived. Unfortunately, though, the likes of Gudeman, Escobar and Polanyi are rather the exception than the rule in economic and development circles, whereby, for example, Chinyika and Paxherbals are such practical exceptions. Indeed, the theoretical field of economic development has been dominated by formal economists and sociologists, at the expense of cultural anthropologists and depth psychologists.

Therefore, in the "global south", where closeness to nature and community is the norm, and the formation of the self is closely interwoven with both, orthodox "north-western" development economics and the accompanying institutional forms have been antithetical to such "southern" worlds. It is time then for development economists and modernizing sociologists generally, and agents of transformation specifically, in the process of activating local communities, to shift perspective and to evolve organizational forms that befit local nature and communities. In the terms of your own community activation, in that respect, you will be engaging consciously in such collective activity, from the ground up. As such social and economic value provides the base and the purpose; is sourced through communal relationships; builds on the culture through trade and accumulation; integrally embedded institutions make a powerful contribution to society. We now turn from a developmental and societal perspective, to disclosing new worlds communally and organizationally, through history making, civic virtue and cultural solidarity, altogether via a path of renewal.

References

Escobar, A. (2008) *Territories of Difference: Place, Movements, Life, Redes.* Durham, NC: Duke University Press.

Gudeman, S. (2001) *The Anthropology of Economy.* Oxford, UK: Blackwell.

Hettne, B. (2009) *Thinking about Development.* London: Zed Books.

Mulgan, G. (2005) *A Sense of Community.* London: Resurgence, p. 172.

Polanyi, K. (2001) *The Great Transformation.* Boston, MA: Beacon.

Schieffer, A. and Lessem, A. (2014) *Integral Development: Realising the Transformative Potential of Individuals, Organisations and Societies.* Abingdon, UK: Routledge.

6 Disclose new worlds

Integral awakening of community activation

Summary of chapter:

1 upheld by virtuous citizenship within your organization or without;
2 enhanced by the cultivating solidarity in your enterprise and/or community;
3 consolidated by disclosing altogether new worlds within or without;
4 altogether involving social, cultural or economic history making, not enterprise;
5 culminating, overall, in fashioning yourselves anew.

Introduction

We now turn, emergent wise, in relation to community activation, from eco-dynamics and development studies, to a *renewed* approach to enterprise, identified by the American-Chilean combination, Spinosa, Dreyfus and Flores (Spinosa, 1997). Their approach to *history making* specifically, and to *Disclosing New Worlds* generally, involves an awakening of social, cultural and economic consciousness. We term such integral renewal, at the level of enterprise, the development of social, economic and cultural – if not also natural – solidarity (see Figure 6.1).

History making

How enterprise is "co-constructed"

In Chapter 5 on vitality of place, we dealt with nature and community at a macro level. Now we turn to the micro enterprise, albeit one embedded in society.

Spinosa, Dreyfus and Flores are not your typical business or management, or even economics oriented, academics. Spinosa is a philosopher at Berkeley in California, and Dreyfus is a management academic at

TENETS NE 3/SE 3
Discursive Community
Disclosing New Worlds

TENETS NE 4/SE4   CORE TENET LG/LE   TENETS NE 2/ SE2
Individuation   *Community*   *Restorative Big Picture*
History Making   *Activation/*   Cultivating Solidarity
                             Truth Quest
              Fashion Ourselves Integrally Anew
                   Dreyfus/Spinoza/Flores

TENETS NE 1/SE 1
Direct Democracy
Virtuous Citizenship

Figure 6.1 Reasoned community activation: key emergent tenets.

MIT in Masschusetts, both in North America, while South America's Fernando Flores, a computer scientist and politician, is a Chilean Senator. Flores studied under Spinosa and Dreyfus when exiled from Chile by the Pinochet regime, because of his association with the late communist President Allende. Together, in the 1990s, philsopher, management consultant and computer scientist/political activist fundamentally redesigned the concept of economic, political and cultural enterprise. As such they drew on the work of the German existential – both phenomenologically (relational) and interpretively (renewal) oriented – philosopher, Martin Heidegger, as opposed to building on the more conventional economic philosophy of Adam Smith.

Your life then, for Heidegger (1978), presents itself in terms of the set of possibilities that you individually and communally are. In other words, a lot of the way your life is is given by the culture you have grown up in, or is simply carried along by a kind of unquestioned horizon of acceptance. But, as Heidegger indicates, you can choose certain possibilities for yourself. So, instead of focusing on the instrumental powers of the entrepreneur, typically exploiting a market need, or indeed on the consumer who allegedly has freedom of economic choice, in disclosing *new worlds* you focus on an existential history-making mode of being and becoming – alongside that of the "virtuous citizen" and the "cultivator of solidarity" – in self-actualizing with your community and society.

Vitality and community

Economists and management theorists, if not also sociologists and social psychologists, produce theories of the firm that depict entrepreneurs in terms of the instrumental *effects* of the entrepreneurial process. They look at an entrepreneur like Richard Branson or Warren Buffett as someone who reallocates – or coordinates – resources and hence enterprises, with a view to optimizing economic benefits.

For Spinosa and his colleagues, such an approach, as taken for example by the management guru Peter Drucker (Drucker, 2007), devalues their "history-making" skills, and orientations. Drucker, in his book *Innovation and Entrepreneurship*, follows the Cartesian approach, for Spinosa and his colleagues, to seeking a theory of entrepreneurship. For Drucker, entrepreneurial innovation is "organized, systematic and rational".

Genuine entrepreneurs, as history makers though, are sensitive to historical questions, like what is the role of money in an era of global terrorism and climate change, not just to pragmatic ones, such as what new market opportunities can we exploit? They change the style of our practices as a whole in a particular community. It is then the entire new "history-making" product or service, set within such a community or communities, not merely the lifestyle of the entrepreneur, and his or her practices, that becomes important.

Producing a historical effect

Overall then, for you, the necessarily transdisciplinary, entrepreneurial skills, set in the context of disclosing new worlds, which are important, are:

- first, innovating by *holding on to some anomaly*;
- second, *bringing the anomaly to bear* on tasks;
- third, *sensing of a world in which the anomaly is central*, and embodying, producing and marketing such in an enterprise within a community;
- fourth, preserving and *testing this new understanding*, in workshops and conversations, to see how it fits with wider communal understandings;
- fifth, *preserving its sensibleness and its strangeness* in the change it produces, reconfiguring the way things happen in a particular domain;
- finally, *ensuring that all involved become in tune* with this embodied conception, so the critical distinctions involved in appreciating the product become manifest in the company's and community's way of life.

The anomalies that Muchineripi held onto for example (see Chapter 1) were *freedom* from hunger, through liberating the community from its hitherto colonized mind, politically, and *enterprise*, in terms of the pursuit of individual initative to benefit the community, economically: hence the *freedom to be enterprising* in order to *profit society*. The way in which all ultimately became involved with such was through the community democracy that the Chinyika women created. Can you then see yourself in that communal light and to that degree? All this, then, is a far cry from the conventional entrepreneur who may make millions of dollars in annual profit, so to speak, but in the process detract from, rather than contribute to, his or her employees' freedom, as he or she outsources production to the Chinese or Indonesian masses.

The introduction of a product that accommodates such history-making becomes like a social movement, whether in the form of a liberation movement in South Africa or a new appreciation for coffee, rendered by and through Starbucks around the world, or indeed, more recently as depicted in *A Good African Story: How a Small Company Built a Global Brand* (Rugasira, 2013). For Uganda's Andrew Rugasira, again socio-politically as well as economically:

> This became my mission and has been my journey for the last eight years. Under the trade not aid banner and a profit-sharing commitment to our farmers, I developed building blocks for a social enterprise based in Uganda. I introduced programmes that would invest in the areas of coffee agronomy support, that would improve crop quality, post-harvest handling, productivity and environmental stewardship, and institutional capacity building through financial literacy training and the development of Savings and Credit Cooperatives for the farmers. My challenge, though, was could an African social enterprise that aspired to empower the community develop into a profitable, global coffee brand.

The virtuous citizen

Civic humanism and community activism

We now turn from the economic to the socio-political, without losing the central thread of history making/disclosing new worlds (see Table 6.1). Anglo-American political science, for Spinosa in fact, has reflected four alternative understandings of democracy since World War II: *majoritarianism*, based on notions of parliamentary sovereignty; *radical or popular democracy*, encouraging the flexible disassembling of political and cultural institutions to encourage the formation of new forms; *civic humanism* which

Table 6.1 Community activation gene: disclosing new spaces

Communal activation: disclosing new worlds emergent path of reasoned realization history making, cultivating solidarity, virtuous citizenship
• *Communal attributes*: grounding – livelihood, healing, truth quest; emergence – permaculture, vitality, *disclosing new worlds*; navigation – participatory, study circles, networks; effect – community building, self-sufficiency, mutual advantage.   • *Integrator role*: community steward, e.g. *Steve Jobs*, Apple; *Luther King*.   • *Communal function*: communal enterprise and development by *fashioning ourselves integrally anew*.   • *Grounded in value*: purpose of *history making*; is sourced through *virtuous citizenship* in a community; builds on the culture through *cultivating solidarity*; at best such communities powerfully contribute to *disclosing new worlds*; at their worst rigid dogma prevails.

takes us back to the Greek polis, as well as to so called communitarianism; and the currently most pervasive democratic form – *liberalism*.

For Spinosa, Dreyfus and Flores' community activism, in their civic terms rather, is the joining together of all, individually and collectively, to promote diverse goods. People with different orderings of goods must thereby work together to produce a space where each with the help of others can develop his or her own good. Because the ancient Greek style of civic humanism, just like that of the members of a traditional African community in Zimbabwe or Nigeria, as we have indicated subordinated, as such, private good to political life (Chapter 2), Spinosa adopts the cause of *civic activism* instead. Where liberal justice tries to distribute resources so that each person can pursue their own good, without government interference, civic activists look for fair distribution of participation and participatory skills, acting skillfully in concert with others to effect change. How then is it different for the engaged, virtuous citizen from the genuine entrepreneur?

What Spinosa has argued, therefore, is that democracy makes better sense in the hands of those like Mai Mlambo in Chinyika (see Chapter 1) or Father Anselm Adodo in Nigeria (see Chapter 2), being, as such, sensitive to concrete anomalies, thereby taking risks, cross-appropriating (that is where the catalytic role of Trans4m comes in), and changing the cultural practices that determine our form of public association. We finally turn to cultural solidarity and thereby reconnect with our individual and collective source.

Cultivators of solidarity

Cultural solidarity, as Spinosa and his collagues define it, is a sense of ultimate responsibility to the most encompassing disclosive space that makes the combined activities, say in the Chinyika case of the entrepreneur (e.g. Muchineripi), the virtuous citizen (e.g. Kada), and the cultivator of such solidarity (e.g. Mlambo), matter altogether.

In other times, historically speaking, poets in Europe or praise singers in Africa, for example, have articulated the meaning of a culture's practices, sharpened its concerns, and thereby transformed our perceptions of the shared "we". This is very much what Father Anselm Adodo (see Chapter 2) has been doing within Edo State, by focusing on community healing. For example, both Mahatma Gandhi in the more distant past and Martin Luther King more recently are also legendary in this regard as cultural figures who in India and the US, respectively, saw people as equals. King was first of all an African American who had experienced the effects of racial inequality and could therefore speak with authority of deep injustices in American life. He was also a Boston University trained theologian. The principle of equality was not just legal dogma in the United States; it expressed the early colonists' sense of the infinite worth of every soul. For King, the retreat from equality was not merely a legal problem but was a falling away from a concern that was fundamental to US culture.

His response – in its honesty, historicity, and fullness – focuses attention on and articulates a defining concern as something people ought to live clearly and coherently. Unlike the entrepreneur, who reconfigures a domain of economic practices, an articulator tries to respond adequately to the communal and culturally central influences on his or her life, and that of his or her community. If there is a disharmony, he or she tries to embody it, as was the case for Steve Kada in Chinyika, seeing to *de-colonize people's minds*. King as such, like Gandhi in India if not also in South Africa hitherto, tried to embody America's inhibited concern for equality, the originating source that makes it sensible, and his current condition in the so-called land of the free.

Conclusion

Disclosing new worlds

Overall, Spinosa and his colleagues have argued for the importance of history-making skills. As such they have cited three history makers – the entrepreneur, the virtuous citizen and the orchestrator of cultural solidarity – altogether providing meaningful lives for citizens, by disclosing new worlds.

The three modes of innovative activity each have the same structure. The entrepreneur, virtuous citizen and orchestrator of culture solidarity each find in their lives something disharmonious that commonsense overlooks or denies. They then hold onto this disharmony, between past and future, individual and community, east and west or north and south, and live with intensity until it reveals how the commonsense way of acting fails. As the source of disharmony became clearer, each of our history makers became a puzzle solver. The only effective way to accomplish such is to be intensely involved with the practices in which he or she dwells that produces anomalies. Their own practices for living, for an Ibrahim Abouliesh as for a Chidara Muchineripi, for a Martin Luther King as for an Anselm Adodo, become the puzzle. They live to find out what they are implicitly taking as important, without prejudging the issue by adducing established formulations for dealing with life.

Fashioning ourselves anew

The entrepreneurs, then, had to ignore rational planning. King had to overcome the sense that he should have been seeking a legal or technocratic solution to the race problem, and was thereby entering into a territory of irrationalism. As all stayed with their puzzles, a marginal practice came to look as though it held more importance in their lives, and in the lives of others, than they had initially supposed. What was at first disturbing for them ultimately helped them make sense of the way their fellow citizens, or immediate community, if not community of interest, lived and worked. The change they established changed, as community activists in different guises, the way all others in the disclosive space encountered things, and everyone therein was put in a place of fashioning themselves anew, albeit that the new was born out of the old.

Cultural solidarity, citizen virtue and entrepreneurship

The cultivation of cultural solidarity, of citizen virtue and of entrepreneurial technological and social innovation, are the activities in which three kinds of world disclosing, and thereby history making, take place. Developing historically laden identity, first, is the job for cultivators of cultural solidarity and the institutions that support them. Second, a civil democracy must occupy itself with structures of association amongst its people. Third, people need to share a disclosive space of ultimate consequence in which they live and work, institutionalizing the innovative, forward looking aspect of entrepreneurial skill.

To what extent then is each of these in evidence, in the course of your community activation, and how therein do you intend to enhance one or another, by virtuous citizenship; cultivating solidarity; disclosing new worlds; and overall history making, thereby fashioning yourself/ourselves integrally anew?

We now turn, with a view to navigating from southern local grounding in ubuntu, communitalism and promocracy, and eastern local-global emergence through permaculture, societal embeddedness and disclosing new worlds, to the northern navigation of community activism, initially via the so-called wealth of networks.

References

Drucker, P. (2007) *Innovation and Entrepreneurship.* London: Routledge.

Heidegger, M. (1978) *Being and Time.* Chichester, UK: Wiley-Blackwell.

Rugasira, A. (2013) *A Good African Story: How a Small Company Built a Global Coffee Brand.* London: Vintage Books.

Spinosa, C., Flores, F. and Dreyfus, F. (1997) *Disclosing New Worlds.* Cambridge, MA: MIT Press.

Part III

Northern communal navigation

Participatory action research, study circles, networks

7   Participatory action research

A research-laden institutional perspective on community activation

Summary of chapter:

1   recognizing community's life world – *vivencia* – in or out of your enterprise;
2   enhancing such via people's self-development organizationally/societally;
3   consolidating upon it by continuously animating the whole community;
4   reinforced though action research, in alternating action and reflection cycles;
5   altogether institutionally combining knowledge and action.

Introduction

Action research as a whole

We now turn, with our continuing pre-emphasis on southern nature and community, from eastern culture and spirituality to now northern research, and knowledge creation, though in overall southern communal guise to participatory action research (PAR), by way now of *navigation* (Figure 7.1).

The founding fathers of such overall *action research* on which PAR is based are the American pragmatic philosopher and educator, John Dewey, and the Jewish refugee from Nazi Germany, the social psychologist Kurt Lewin – in the middle of the last century. Action research – for one of its contemporary co-creators Peter Reason in England, together with Hilary Bradbury based in California is:

> [a] participatory, democratic process concerned with developing practical knowing in the pursuit of worthwhile human purposes, grounded in a participatory worldview which is believed to be emerging at this historical moment. It seeks to bring together action

TENETS LG3/LE 3/LT 3
Build Up Social Capital
Cultural, Political and Economic Commonwealth
Community Animation

TENETS LG 4/LE 4/LT 4	CORE TENET LG/LE/LT	TENETS LG 2/LE 2/LT2
Community Ownership	*Community*	*Add Natural Value*
Great Work of Nature	*Activation/*	*Heal the Earth*
Action Research	**Secure Livelihood**	People's Selfdevelopment
	Permaculture	

Institutionally Combine Action & Knowledge
Nyerere, Ouédraogo, Fals Borda, Rahmen

TENETS LG1/LE 1/L1
Underlying Ubuntu
Pursue Earth Justice
Vivencia

Figure 7.1 Relational community activation: navigational tenets.

and reflection, theory and practice, in participation with others, in the pursuit of practical solutions to issues of pressing concern to people, and more generally the flourishing of individual persons and their communities.

(Reason and Bradbury, 2004)

Action research to PAR

We now turn specifically to *participatory* action research (PAR), which is the overall research orientation and indeed approach to action research most closely aligned with community activation. We first then introduce you to its origins and initial development (see Table 7.1).

The Colombian sociologist Orlando Fals Borda, who has since become a leading light in the PAR movement, had been working on the same alternative approach to social research but without being aware of the international initiatives that had been taking place in the previous years. He and his colleagues, now based at the University of British Columbia in Vancouver, were still using the generic term *action research*. Its originator had argued that research that produced nothing but books was not sufficient, and that a new type of research for social practice was needed. Thus, he called for

Table 7.1 Participatory CARE

Communal activation: participatory navigating the relational path combining action and knowledge

- *Communal attributes*: south – ubuntu, primal, communitalism; east – organic, vitality, solidarity; north – networks, study circles, *participatory*; west – community building, self-sufficiency, mutual aid.
- *Integrator role*: community steward, e.g. *Julius Nyerere*, Tanzanian President; Columbian sociologist *Orlando Fals Borda* (also a catalyst); *Bernard Lédéa Ouédraogo* and the Six Ss in the Sahel.
- *Communal function*: communal learning and development through which communities *institutionally combine knowledge and action.*
- *Grounded in value*: the community's *vivencia* (life world) provides the value base; builds on the culture through *people's self-development*; navigated via *animating a community*; activated and transformed through ongoing *action research* at best making a powerful contribution to development of society; at worst such knowledge/energy dissipates.

"a type of action research on the conditions and effects of various forms of social action, and research leading to social action".

At an action research conference in 1977, the concept of *action research* used by Fals Borda met the concept of *participatory research* previously coined, and *participatory action research* was later born. The term was used for the first time by Orlando Fals Borda to name a new paradigm in social research. Several decades later, the concept became popularized and known by its initials PAR. We now turn to PAR's key tenets as a participatory research methodology that indeed fosters community activation, albeit that it goes all the way, collectively speaking, from origination to transformation.

Combining action and knowledge

A problem is defined, analyzed and solved by the community

For Columbia's renegade academic, Orlando Fals Borda (Fals Borda, 1991), learning to interact and organize with PAR is based on the orientation towards experience proposed by the Spanish philosopher Jose Ortega y Gasset. Through the actual experience of something, for him, we intuitively apprehend its essence; we feel, enjoy and understand it as a reality, and we thereby place our own being in a wider, more fulfilling communal context. In PAR, such an experience, called *vivencia* (akin to life world and aligned to learning with head and heart) in Spanish, is complemented by another idea, that of authentic commitment. In that context, both internal and external animators or agents of change have shared goals.

A dialectical tension, then, is created between an academic orientation combined with a practical one, bringing together academic and popular knowledge in shared problem solving (Figure 7.2). Through participation, a subject/subject relationship replaces the hitherto asymmetrical subject/ object researcher/researched relationships. The general concept of authentic participation as defined here is *rooted in cultural traditions of the common people and in their real history referring to core values* that have survived the destructive impact of foreign invasions. Such resistant values are based on mutual aid, the communal use of the land, forest and water, the extended family and other old social practices, the endogenous experiences of the common people.

As a scientific methodology, facilitates an analysis of social reality

For Fals Borda, action and knowledge go hand in hand. Historical experience calls for rethinking the meaning of people's liberation. The dominant view of such liberation has been preoccupied with the need for

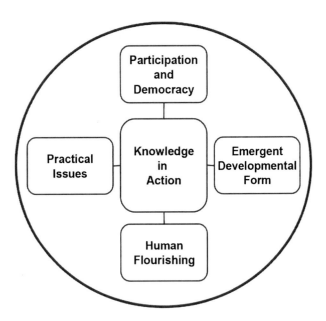

Figure 7.2 Knowledge in action.

changing the oppressive structures of relations in material production – certainly a necessary task. But, and this is the distinctive view of PAR, domination of elites is also rooted in control over social power to determine what is useful knowledge. In fact, existence of the gap in knowledge relations can offset the advantages of reducing the gap in relations of physical production.

People then cannot be liberated by a consciousness and knowledge other than their own. It is therefore essential that people develop their own indigenous consciousness-raising and knowledge generation, and this requires the social power to assert this. The scientific character or objectivity of knowledge rests on its social verifiability, and this depends on consensus as to the method of verification. All scientific knowledge is relative to the paradigm to which it belongs, and the verification system to which it is submitted. An immediate objective of PAR is to return to the all too often poor and deprived people the control over their own verification systems.

PAR is aimed at the exploited, the poor, the oppressed, the marginal

Stimulation of the poor and deprived to undertake self-reliant initiatives requires two essential steps. The first is the development of an awareness about the reality in which they live. In particular, they need to understand that poverty and deprivation are the result of specific social forces rather than an outcome of some inherent deficiency on their part or even "fate". Second, based on such critical awareness, they need to gain confidence in their collective abilities to bring about positive changes in their life situations and organize themselves for that purpose.

PAR creates awareness of the people's own resources

A typical PAR program, therefore, stimulates direct social analysis by the landless. In many places, this had led to intense and sustained pressure-group action to confront social injustice and oppression by rural elites. In other areas, confrontational activity to resist social oppression by rural elites had been particularly intense for several years and had led to many forms of harassment, both of the landless leaders and NGO workers:

- What was their experience?
- What did they learn themselves from this?
- What would they, with their past experience, advise the landless in other villages who might want to get organized?

- What was the relation of their present activities with past ones?
- Would they like to document their story, draw its lessons more systematically after thorough discussion in the base of the organization, and disseminate them so that fellow landless in other villages would not need to start from zero and could benefit from their experience?

PAR involves the full and active participation of the community

Overall, in PAR, there is a break-up of the classical dichotomy between *subject* and *object* (manipulation and dominance) and its replacement by a humanistic mode of equal relation between two subjects (animation and facilitation). The essential difference between the latter approach and that typically undertaken by a political party or conventional development practitioner, in moving from analysis to transformation, is:

- *Starting from where people are* – their perceptions, knowledge, experiences and rhythm of work and thoughts, as opposed to preconceived agendas.
- *Stimulating people (animation) to undertake self-analysis* of their life situations, and helping them to derive from such self-inquiry into the political-economic-cultural environment an intellectual base for initiating changes.
- *Assisting people to organize themselves* into people's organizations (POs) which are non-hierarchical in structure and democratic in operations.
- *Facilitating the actions for change*, with the external catalyst paving the way for internal self-reliance.
- Stimulating the POs to carry out *regular self-reviews*, to assess and learn from success and failure.

The ultimate goal is the radical transformation of social reality

What then is the ultimate goal of all this? For Orlando Fals Borda, those involved in PAR start with the thesis that science does not have absolute or pure value, but is simply a useful form of knowledge for specific purposes and based on relative truths. Any science as a cultural product carries those biases and values, which scientists hold as a group. It therefore favours those who produce and control it. Table 7.2 shows the ingredients and techniques of a people's science.

A people's science may hence serve as a corrective. Ideally, in the process, the grassroots are able to participate in the research-and-innovation

Table 7.2 Ingredients and techniques of a people's science

Ingredients and techniques of a people's science	
Collective research	Dialogue, discussion, argument and consensus in the investigation of social realities.
Critical recovery of history	To discover, selectively through collective memory, popular stories and oral traditions *fleshed out* serving to recover history.
Valuing and applying folk culture	Account is taken of art, music, drama, sports, story-telling and other expressions related to human sentiment and imagination.
Production and diffusion of new knowledge	Different levels of communication are developed for people ranging from pre-literate to intellectual, using image, sound, painting, theatre, music, puppetry. The groups involved include cooperatives, trade unions, cultural centres.

process from the beginning: that is from the moment it is decided what the subject of the research should be, to the time it is completed.

Its essence is the proposition that more is to be gained by using the affective logic of the heart than the cold-headed analyses that come from laboratories. We now turn from Columbian sociologist, Fals Borda, to Bangladeshi Educationalist M.D. Rahman.

People's self-development and transformation

Integrating education with life processes

Like many other of his compatriots, M.D. Rahman (Rahman, 1993) had been inspired by popular mobilizations for social reconstruction and development in Bangladesh after its independence in 1971. As a teacher, Rahman had been stimulated by demands from sections of Bangladesh's student community for radical reform to integrate educational processes with processes of life. Yet most of the popular initiatives in the country faded, died or were repressed as reactionary forces gradually consolidated their hold on society's commanding structures. Joining the ILO (International Labour Organization) in 1977, Rahman was able to pursue the same interest, linking up with significant trends in the grassroots movements in several countries and initiating methodological experiments in field "animation" work and in the sensitization of animators; linking with intellectual trends; working with popular movements; and in synthesizing and conceptualizing from the ongoing experiences.

Organizing the rural poor

According to Rahman, organizing the rural poor, for an NGO, can have several different objectives:

Economic uplift: This means raising the incomes of the poor, giving them greater stability of income, and some social security or insurance against unforeseen situations, old age, and so on. If this is the only or the principal objective, external delivery of such can be in the form of credit, technology and expertise. But emphasis on external delivery contradicts with the other objectives.

Human development: Creativity is the distinctive human quality, for Rahman, and the human development objective aims to develop creative people. Creation is the product of thinking and action that is participation.

Achieving social and economic rights: The means of elimination of economic and social oppression, and achieving equity in the use of public resources, implies the exercise of collective power of the poor and often implies *struggle*. The role of outsiders is to help develop a consciousness amongst the poor of short-run failures as a learning process upon which subsequent strategy is to be built.

Macro-social transformation: The above three objectives can be considered to be *locally progressive* if they are pursued together, that is progressive at a micro level. Their contribution to macro social transformation can be positive, if such micro work spreads on a broad enough scale. Since the great bulk of the flow of external resources is controlled by external forces, interested (according to Rahman) in dominating and exploiting the country rather than in its self-determination and development, a self-reliant development effort is an absolutely necessary element for the country to shape its own destiny and stand up with pride. We now turn, by way of conclusion, to the most prominent historical example of PAR in practice, which sadly though faded away once its key protagonists were no longer involved.

Conclusion: PAR as a social movement

PAR and the Six Ss in the Sahel

What, then, is the significance of PAR as a macro-level social transformation? Possibly the largest such institutional movement, at least in the early nineties, was the so-called six Ss ("Se Servir de la Saison Sèche en Savane et au Sahel") in Burkino Faso, which covered about two-thirds of the country's villages, as well as those of adjacent West African countries

(Pradervand, 1990). It was founded in 1976 by Bernard Ouédraogo with the French development expert Bernard Lecomte, the former becoming its Executive Director two years later.

Bernard Lédéa Ouédraogo, a core initiator of the *Six S* movement, was born in Upper Volta (now Burkina Faso) in 1930. He completed his secondary education there and gained numerous diplomas. Ouédraogo then became a teacher and school director before he then turned to agriculture, where his talents as a trainer led him to the top echelons of the civil service. But he found he was unable to help the farmers and village groups whom he was supposed to be training, so he left to find out why. Studying in France, he obtained a doctorate from the Sorbonne in 1977 in the Social Sciences of Development.

His first question, while he was undertaking his doctorate, was whether anything existed in the traditional society of the Mossi (Burkina's largest ethnic group) that resembled village groups.

> We undertook a thorough study of village social organization – the people's thinking and their social and economic structures – and we discovered that the Naam group, a traditional village body composed of young people, had the most highly developed cooperative character-istics. We decided we would attempt to work with the Naam structures.

The result was an initiative unique in Africa. Despite a lot of problems, the Naam groups prospered. By 1978 there were over 2,500 groups in Yatenga province with 160,000 members. Twenty years later this had risen to 6,480 groups all over Burkina Faso and adjoining countries – almost half of them women's groups – with a membership of 300,000. The transformation of the traditional Naam groups into modern social structures was a brilliant piece of practical sociology by Ouédraogo.

More recently, Six S has undergone some restructuring and has sadly lost its way, ultimately failing to institutionalize PAR. In the mid-1990s, Ouédraogo was elected Mayor of his hometown, Ouahigouya. Beside the success of Six S, he is doubtful of the future: "The danger for many Africans is that the erosion of our ways by the aggressive ways of others, our own values by foreign values, will destroy our sense of responsibility for solving our communities' problems".

Reflecting on "what is development?"

People's collective self-development initiatives, for Fals Borda, as was the case for Ouedraogo and may be the case for you, not only point to a way out of the development impasse. They also suggest the need for reflection on the very notion of development. For a long time, as we pointed out in

Chapter 5, development has been associated with the mechanistic notion of the development of physical assets and increasing the flow of economic and social goods and services. Much of the activities articulated here are developmental, but questions remain as to whether the process of people mobilizing themselves is a means of development or an end in itself.

Genuine people-oriented activists seldom come from the professional classes. However, people with a powerful societal vision, conception, intellectual ability and methodological skill for translating conception into practice are needed to provide some guidance and perspective for such initiatives, and for these to spread widely with some coherence. People seem to be ready to respond to such animation. Must this be left to spontaneous historical emergence, or can some method of "schooling" be devised to promote a greater concern among a nation's potential intellectual leaders to work with and not upon the people, so that the "other Africa" could develop faster?

Praxis and the recovery of history and culture

Participative action research, in conclusion, has demonstrated in concrete cases its ability to further the progress of the grassroots rather then the vested interests of dominant groups. As such, the rediscovery of cultural roots is an essential element in any effort to improve depressed communities.

The more important practical challenge PAR faces, for Fals Borda, is the need of common people to articulate in social movements, along with new knowledge, the necessary political struggles for justice and progress. As such, we are discovering once more the pertinence of participatory action research to the transformation of our societies into a more satisfactory and less violent world. However, as the Six Ss' case has illustrated, failure to fully institutionalize such will inhibit the long-term effectiveness of such participatory research. Altogether then a community's life world (vivencia) is enhanced through the people's self-development, consolidated upon by animating the community, reinforced though action research, altogether and institutionally combining knowledge and action. We now turn from participatory action research to study circles, and as such from "*south*-north" to "*north*-south" as far as community activation is concerned.

References

Fals Borda, O. (ed) (1991) *Action and Knowledge.* New York: Apex Publishing.
Pradervand, P. (1990) *Listening to Africa – Developing Africa from the Grassroots.* New York: Praeger.
Rahman, M.D. (1993) *People's Self Development.* London: Zed Books.
Reason, P. and Bradbury, H. (2004) *Handbook of Action Research.* London: Sage.

8 Study circles

An educational and institutional research perspective on community activation

Summary of chapter:

1 based on participants' genuine interest in individual and collective learning;
2 enhanced by the informal character of the study circles;
3 navigated thought a flexible framework to support learning and development;
4 resulting in collective learning, of through person, community, organization;
5 effected through institutionalized study circles spread across community and society.

Introduction

Swedish origins of the study circles

We now turn from Africa and Asia to the heart of Europe, that is, to the tiny country located at Europe's cross-roads, Slovenia, with which we have been intimately engaged now for several years, in co-evolving what we have termed *Integral Green Slovenia*.

We also turn from research-based community activation, relationally speaking, to education and learning, on the path of renewal, now focused on emancipatory navigation (Figure 8.1).

Spearheaded by a citizens' initiative, coordinated by a civil servant and developmental educator, Darja Piciga (Piciga *et al.*, 2016), the story of Slovenia's knowledge-based development consists of a multitude of cases, some of them taking place in small communities, some of them spreading across the entire country. Their intertwinement and mutual support – as in the specific case of a network of study circles and the local community

TENETS NG3/NE 3/NT 3
Combining Nature, Spirit, Science, Economy
Socially Embedded Institutions
Flexible Framework

TENETS NG 4/NE 4/NT 4   CORE TENET LG/LE/NT   TENETS NG 2/NE 2/NT 2
Communitalism   *Community*   *Fusing Work and Prayer*
Trade and Accumulation   *Activation/*   *Communal Relationships*
Collective Learning   **Heal Community**   Informal Character
                        Vitality of Place
                   Institutionalized Study Circles

TENETS NG1/NE 1/NT 1
Nature Power
Value Base
Genuine Interest

Figure 8.1 Renewed community activation: navigational tenets.

Solčavsko – are cases in point. In fact, developmental and social, culture-based and knowledge-based, communities and economies come together.

Human-centred study circles in fact, as opposed to technology-centred networks, were originally developed and thereby institutionalized in Sweden – culturally, politically, educationally. As such, for American political scientist Leonard Oliver, from the end of the ninteenth century onwards, they formed a public sphere for recurrent meetings of citizens with common interests who formed a unique pattern of communication (Oliver, 1987). The study circle's free, open and permissive milieu of dialogue between equals, who exchanged ideas and experiences with respect to each other and without limits, was well suited to the efforts aimed at achieving fundamental human rights in society. Human rights were exercised in such group circles since, at the same time, they were demanded in a community as a whole. In a sense, in this *northern* expression of communal activation, the pedagogical context seemed to work to enoble/refine the social capital and common values necessary for a well-functioning modern society.

Roots in popular Swedish movements

More specifically for Oliver then, Oscar Olssen, early last century, a leader of Sweden's temperance movement, developed the study circle as a means of popular education. Other socially conscious movements followed suit, including the blue-collar unions, the consumer cooperatives, and the Swedish Social Democratic Party (SAP), as well as the nonconformist church, for which study circles provided an effective means of recruiting and educating their members. What was learned in the study circle subsequently carried over into political life, as most of the popular movements eventually became active in political affairs. Materials published encouraged workers to "gain the knowledge necessary to master public issues, to understand how society works, to take control of their lives, and to master the tools to change society".

Such study materials were supplemented, and also thereby institutionalized, by materials from "People's Libraries", created throughout Sweden by the temperance groups and labour organizations long before municipalities extended their library facilities outside the cities. Today, these ten national associations that sponsor study circles emphasize cultural studies (languages, literature, the arts), rather than the political, social and economic issues (civic affairs) that dominated study circles in earlier times.

Sweden today has ten national educational associations, which promote, organize and conduct study circles with government subsidies. A leading example is the Worker's Educational Association (ABF), the largest study circle association, which is focused on blue-collar industrial unions, consumer cooperatives and the SAP (Swedish Social Democratic Party). It has 43 affiliated organizations, publishes its own magazine and takes positions on national education and cultural policies. In fact, this link to national associations is key to the success of the study circle movement. The trade unions alone employ over 60,000 study organizers, many carrying out study circle recruitment at the workplace with employer approval and on company time. These organizers are responsible for over 150,000 study circles annually for trade union members, almost half of those in the country. The system seems to work with almost three million adult Swedes in the late 1980s (today there are nine-and-a-half million Swedes in total) participating annually in study circles.

Slovenian study circles and the process of democratization

The Scandinavian model of study circles according to Slovenian educationalists Gougoulakis and Nevenka Bogataj (Gougoulakis and Bogataj, 2007), was introduced into the country in 1991 in order to contribute to the democratization of society and to develop adult education. The main development agent was the Slovenian Institute for Adult Education (SIAE). The main components of Slovenian study circles are: a non/hierarchical, action oriented, trained leadership of a locally rooted mentor and a sense of togetherness amongst the participants with a common shared goal set in the communicative process (see Table 8.1). This indeed is a form of community activation, *northern* style. A study circle integrates individual and group initiatives by the establishment of the "common", including personal responsibility, overcoming the lack of intermediary bodies in post-modern society. This form of community activation moreover serves to build up social capital. Another role – building the ties of the community with the local natural environment – is more common in rural environments.

Four components combine to make up the concept of the study circle in Slovenia, namely, the *loose framework, the informal character of the study situation, the collective learning environment* and *the participants' genuine interest in knowledge*. Social capital becomes acquired at the very moment the participants are in a communicative relationship with each other, and it is composed of knowledge, abilities and competences for a meaningful life, as well as in public and private life. In recent years, moreover, the aim of study circles in Slovenia has changed from an initial emphasis on democratization in Slovenia to their more recent focus on local community development. The most frequently selected topic during the entire period of their functioning is identity and heritage – regardless of dichotomy of aims (e.g. personal/local learning), types of participants (retired/employed) and effects (most effective are considered those study circles who use local history as means of community activation).

With such circles, for adult educator Nevenka Bogata (Bogata, 2013) areas are thus provided with a rare opportunity for self-organized learning which – by design – has to end with a local event or issue. Considerable contributions of study circles to local contexts are regularly recognized on a local and state level, occasionally also on a European Union level. Circles are interpreted as a first phase of development, where motivation

Table 8.1 CARE circles in Slovenia

Communal activation: study circles navigation of renewal path contribution to development through learning
• *Communal attributes*: grounding – livelihood, healing; east – permaculture, vitality, new worlds; north – networks, *study circles*, participatory; west – community building, self-sufficiency, mutual aid.
• *Integrator role*: community steward, e.g. *Marko Slapnik, Solčavsko.*
• *Communal function*: communal development: build up of *social capital.*
• *Grounded in value*: is sourced through *participants' genuine interest in learning*; builds on the culture through *informal character*; navigates through a *flexible framework* to systematize a sustainable purpose; at best such circles make a powerful contribution to society through *institutionalized collective learning*; at their worst dogma prevails.

and a common goal development are very important. In fact, study circles have considerably contributed to the development of sustainable tourism and developmental, culture-based economy – as was the case for Solčavsko, a remote alpine municipality in Slovenia.

Supporting regional development in Slovenia: study circles at Solčavsko

Towards sustainable development

Situated along the state border, distant from large urban areas, Solčavsko is the case of a relatively small municipality whose population is linked through study circles in a very functional way. For the community, sustainable developmental practices are of particular interest to bring forth a culture-based economy that considers tradition an essential pillar of development. Its practice of local development started long ago as this is a medieval settlement with a historically unique development path.

A series of study circles, in cooperation with the Slovenian Institute for Adult education, was instrumental for Solčavsko's most recent development, towards a fully fledged integral development model, drawing on nature and culture, technology and economy, but with a primary focus on nature- and heritage-based tourism. This process influenced, over time, the setting up of Center Rinka, which became the main institutional driver of Solčavsko's holistic approach. The Center resulted from the initiative of visionary local citizens, dedicated to their environment and heritage. Under the leadership of its former director Marko Slapnik (Lešnik Štuhec and Slapnik, 2014), Center Rinka became a role model for an integrated local development agency. In Figure 8.1 we illustrated how the integral development framework can explain the case of Solčavsko. Participating in the activities of the Citizens' Initiative for Integral Green Slovenia helped Slapnik to connect all key elements of their local development model. At the very core of the model is a deep belief, held by the local population, seeing nature, not man, as the ultimate change-agent; subsequently, the Solčavsko model subordinates each developmental activity to the primacy of conserving and respecting nature.

Building on Solčavsko's nature and tradition

The Solčavsko region is located at the upper current of the Savinja River along the Slovenian-Austrian border. The area is surrounded by a mountain chain of the Kamnik-Savinja Alps and Karavanks. Solčavsko consists of three Alpine glacial valleys: Logarska dolina, Robanov kot and Matkov kot.

In the middle of the area lies a small village of Solčava with some dozens of inhabitants while the whole municipality has up to only about 600 people. The area is 103 square kilometres large, but there are an average of only 5 inhabitants per square kilometre. More than 80 per cent of the area is under protection. In the Solčavsko region, tourism remains closely connected with traditional activities: agriculture, forestry and handicrafts. For centuries, the largest farms in the whole Alpine space have existed here and remained more or less self-sufficient. Solčavsko then is characterized by eco-tourism. There are (intentionally) no large ski lifts. The mentality of resolute and persistent locals is therefore a particular feature of Solčavsko and one could say that the community is at the same time cohesive and open. The proof is that annually more than 100,000 visitors come, drawn by the natural beauty and recreation possibilities that the region offers, but also for the excellence of its facilities.

Initiating study circles at Solčavsko

Study circles at Solčavsko's Panoramic Road in 2004 focused on learning for tourism development in the context of protection of natural and cultural heritage. They resulted in the development and editing of promotional materials, a local dictionary and typical food recipes. Study circles, as a form of community activism, proved to be not only an investment into internal cohesion through dialogue-based learning but also a stimulation of targeted activities, provided to the municipality as project ideas.

Sustainability as the key to Solčavsko's development

Solčavsko's sustainability orientation has been significantly strengthened in two respects: first, through the release of internal innovation potential, and second, through external expert support. Both elements are regarded as crucial in its approach to study circles and were significantly strengthened by their direct link and constant dialogical exchange. The first one, innovation potential, is best represented by the name of a local inhabitant, Avgust Lenar, who provided a new governance model. Lenar, a forester by profession, but since 1992 Solčavsko's Landscape Park (Logarska dolina Ltd) Manager describes the region's developmental path as follows:

> In the 80s of the 20th century, farmers in Logarska dolina had several problems with many careless visitors parking in a natural environment, setting up fires, littering and causing damage to the environment and locals in different ways. In 1987, the municipality created a Landscape Park. However, there were no control services and money

for development. Therefore, the landowners established a company in 1992 and obtained a concession for the management of the park. They started to collect entrance fees for motor vehicles. It was the first such example in Slovenia where locals managed the park, which first aroused disapproval from visitors and the professional community. But the awards and a wide recognition for the successful management of the protected area soon confirmed that the decisions of the locals had been correct.

Second, the efforts of the local shareholders and a unique management style of Landscape Park Logarska dolina have been supported by many experts. Among them, Boštjan Anko and Jernej Stritih have greatly contributed to the development of the Park and to the broader understanding of protected areas. Anko (Anko *et al.*, 2007) wrote:

> For the last two or three generations, the locals of Solčavsko have seen their chance to survive and their future in self-sufficient farming, market-oriented livestock production, income from the forest, mass tourism, ecotourism . . . The whole future development should be seen as a collection of the best of what each of the above activities has to offer. Finding the future will not be oriented towards finding a single "ideal" activity, but towards finding a harmonious coexistence of all of these activities (which are part of Solčavsko identity) – and some more – on the basis of sustainable thinking. Stability and strength of Highland people and their farms lies in their conservatism, and their mistrust towards novelties which leave little room for manoeuvre for correcting mistakes in unfavourable natural conditions.

How then did Solčavsko manage to align its diverse and geographically dispersed population under a common goal? Again, study circles played a crucial role.

Connecting people via common goals/seeking development opportunities

Common goals and seeking development opportunities are a constant challenge for any distant entity. Solčavsko started to test study circles. Their first study circle (mentored by the district forester Alojz Lipnik) was provided in the upper area of the valley, to scattered farms along Panorama Road, aimed at preservation, revival and development of the natural, cultural and ethnological heritage of the area. Following its positive experience and outcomes, several other circles developed later with clear purpose and creative energy among people who up to then did not contribute their time and effort to the evolution of the common goal.

The results were inspiring. An NGO, called "Society for the Development and Conservation of Natural and Cultural Heritage Panorama" was established. It carried out a project preserving the heritage at Solčavsko Panoramic Road already in its first year and received a Ford Foundation award, given to visionary leaders and organizations on the frontlines of social change worldwide, for its outcomes. Alojz Lipnik, later elected mayor of Solčavsko, continued to use the principles and methodology of study circles for connecting people with common goals and seeking development opportunities for locals in the municipality of Solčava. He emphasized listening as the basis of co-operation and intergenerational flow.

Lipnik stressed that:

> The experience of study circles is extremely valuable as well as knowing that it is necessary to listen to the people around you. Young people need help of their seniors to use their talents, knowledge and skills in order to find business opportunities in their hometown.

The main result of the municipality's multiple activities was the establishment of the public institution Center Rinka, aimed at managing visitors and introducing them into sustainable management of human and natural resources.

A multipurpose centre for the sustainable development of Solčavsko

Visitor management is a tool for sustainable tourism development in the natural environment: Center Rinka was established in the village of Solčava upon this principle.

Slapnik (Croft, 2014) explains:

> Institution Center Rinka encourages the development of local products in many different ways. But the main topics are always wood-, wool- and food-production. All the events and activities at Center Rinka are held in close connection with local people, tourism providers and visitors of Solčavsko. Solčavsko remains a community of creative people with a clear development vision. We also involve young, educated locals with new projects, trying to help them in finding business opportunities and creating green jobs.

In the Solčavsko case, we can also recognize the globally disseminated success formula: "Dreaming – planning – doing – celebrating are the four steps needed for successful work" (Piciga *et al.*, 2016).

A public institution was established in order to create the contents and management of Center Rinka and to provide support to locals in the field of tourism and sustainable development. The main idea or mantra always repeated is: "Local material, local people, local skills and knowledge" (Lešnik Štuhec and Slapnik, 2014).

Conclusion: integrally into the future

Based on knowledge, experience and tradition

If we take a concluding look at Solčavsko as a specific illustration of an Integral Green Economy (Figure 8.2), in recent decades co-evolved through study circles as a form of community activation, we can see in the moral core our response to "the good of the community". In this core, there is also

Figure 8.2 Solčavsko in the frame of integral green economy.

Source: Designed by Darja Piciga and Marko Slapnik.

a lot of interest and motivation to take action for the good of the community and for its development – motivation to take action for the common good instead of as shallow focus on individual good.

The approach of taking small and moderate steps towards innovation is common in Slovenia's Alpine region. At the same time, there is a strong connection between nature and culture, including a commitment to a sustainable life style. Small and moderate steps of innovation, education and also research provide continuation and materialization of the moral core and accommodation to a sustainable life style for those who are willing to follow the Solčavsko model.

Project-based study circles

Activities in study circles have encouraged the development of sustainability oriented projects: like the setting up of tourist facilities around the Solčava Panoramic Road and the Mountain Wood Festival. For Marko Slapnik, the former director of Center Rinka, the people of Solčavsko as a community want to stay in touch with nature, cultural identity and with each other. He is convinced that its integral developmental model is not only the right solution for Solčavsko, but also presents an opportunity for a wider area of Upper Savinja Valley and other communities in the Alpine space.

Overall then, study circles are based on participants' genuine interest, enhanced by their informal character, navigated through the flexible framework supporting them, resulting in institutionalized collective learning in Sweden as well as in Slovenia. What role, overall, do you feel such study circles have to play in your own community activation?

We now turn from research and education, aligned with community activation, to technology based institutionalized research and networked communications.

References

Anko, B., Anteric, M., Clarke, R., Koščak, M., Lenar, A., Mitchell, I. and Slapnik, M. (2007) *Študije o Solčavskem 1932–2007*. Poročilo o skupnem terenskem delu Univerze v Ljubljani in Univerze v Londonu. Solčava: Občina Solčava in Logarska dolina d.o.o.

Bogataj, N. *et al.* (2013) *Študijski krožki kot prispevek k razvoju lokalne skupnosti*. Radeče: JZ KTRC, Ljubljana, Slovenia: DTP.

Croft, J. (2014) *Skupina predanih ljudi lahko spremeni svet*. Interview in newspaper Delo, Slovenia. www.delo.si/zgodbe/sobotnapriloga/skupina-predanih-ljudi-lahko-spremeni-svet.html (accessed September 2014).

Gougoulakis, P. and Bogataj, N. (2007) 'Study circles in Sweden and Slovenia: Learning for civic participation'. In Adam, F. (ed.) *Social Capital and Governance: Old and New Members of the EU in Comparison*. Berlin: Lit Verlag.

Lešnik Štuhec, T. and Slapnik, M. (2014) Vključenost deležnikov v lokalne dobaviteljske verige turističnih in s turizmom povezanih produktov na Solčavskem. In Mušič, K., Kociper, T. and Sikošek, M. (eds) *Turizem in management. Na poti k uspešni poslovni prihodnosti. Koper: Založba Univerze na Primorskem*, pp. 481–493. Available at: www.hippocampus.si/ISBN/978-961-6832-79-3.pdf (accessed September 2014).

Oliver, L. (1987) *Study Circles: Coming Together for Personal Growth and Change*. Washington, DC: Seven Locks Press.

Piciga, D., Schieffer, A. and Lessem, R. (2016) *Integral Green Slovenia Economy and Society*. Abingdon, UK: Routledge.

9 Wealth of networks

A networked and institutionalized research perspective on community activation

Summary of chapter:

1 providing underlying commons laden purpose to your community/ organization;
2 enhanced through peer-to-peer-based research and networking;
3 building socially, technically and institutionally via open source connectivity;
4 resulting in institutionalized research networks, communally/ organizationally;
5 culminating with your individual and collective role in an information society.

Introduction

Information society

Finally, by way of "northern navigation", involving science and technology, systems and knowledge creation, of community activation, you turn from participatory action research (relational path) and study circles (renewal path) to information and communication networks (path of reasoned realization) (Figure 9.1). For us moreover, if not also for you, the course of history moves back and forth in circles, and spins spirals hither and thither, as much as it might follow lines of progress and focus on specific goals or points. Along the way, nature and community, culture and consciousness, and now more explicitly science and technology, each have their role to play.

In such a context, for legal scholar Yochai Benkler (Benkler, 2006), Berkman Professor of Entrepreneurial Legal Studies at Harvard Law School, knowledge and culture are central to human freedom and development. How they are produced and exchanged, for example in America

TENETS NE 3/SE 3/SN 3
Discursive Community
Disclosing New Worlds
Open Source

TENETS NE 4/SE 4/SN 4	CORE TENET LG/LE/SN	TENETS NE 2/ SE 2/ SN 3
Individuation	*Community*	*Restorative Big Picture*
History Making	*Activation/*	*Cultivating Solidarity*
Institutionalized Networks	**Truth Quest**	Peer-to-Peer
	Fashioning Ourselves Anew	
	Information Society	

TENETS NE 1/SE 1/SN 1
Direct Democracy
Virtuous Citizen
Natural & Social Commons

Figure 9.1 Reasoned community activation: navigational tenets.

globally, in the same way as how they are developed, in Chinyika locally, critically affects the state of the economy. How then are knowledge and culture produced and exchanged in the context of your own community activation?

For what characterizes the newly emerging networked information economy is that decentralized individual and communal action – carried out through radically distributed, nonmarket mechanisms, plays a much greater role than it did, or could have, in the industrial information economy.

The alter-modern economy

Through the rise of such non-market pre-industrial or post-industrial production then, individuals and communities can reach and inform thousands, for example in the Chinyika communal case (see Chapter 1), and millions, in the internet virtual case. Ultimately then, effective, large-scale cooperative efforts, that is peer production of information, knowledge and culture, are on the rise. As such, up to 300,000 villagers in and around Chinyika can be communally activated, as are millions of us using the internet and social networking sites worldwide. Whereas one is local and "high-touch" (Chinyika) and the other global and "high-tech" (internet), the mode of co-production associated with each is the same.

Table 9.1 CARE for networks

Communal activation: networks institutional navigation of the path of reasoned realization extending the social research commons
• *Communal attributes*: grounding – livelihood, healing, truth quest; emergence – permaculture, vitality of place, disclosing new worlds; north –participatory, study circles, *networks*; west – community building, self-sufficiency, mutual advantage. • *Integrator role*: community steward, e.g. *Stallman – Gnu, Torvalds – Linux, Shuttleworth – ubuntu software*. • *Communal function*: communal learning and development whereby communities are lodged in the social and virtual *information society*. • *Grounded in value*: value provides the *commons laden* purpose; is sourced through *peer-to-peer relationships* in a community; builds on the *open source* connectivity; at best communities are enriched via *a wealth of institutionalized networks*; at worst chaos prevails.

In both the pre- and post-industrial networked information economies, furthermore, the physical capital required for production is broadly distributed throughout society. In North America, this occurs interpersonally via personal computers and virtual networks. In Chinyika, if not also around Paxherbals, this arises communally, through families and clan networks. According to Benkler, "We are in the midst of a technological, economic and organizational transformation that allows us to renegotiate the terms of freedom, justice and productivity in the past-future information society". How we shall live in this new environment will in some significant measure depend on policy choices we make, in the "north" and in the "south", in the next decade or so (see Table 9.1).

An economic policy, allowing yesterday's winners, whether Microsoft in America or Anglo-American in Africa, to dictate the terms of tomorrow's economic competition, for Benkler, would be disastrous, in the US as well as in Zimbabwe, though the policy choices are somewhat different in each case. So what does this imply for your duly networked community activation?

Information production and community activism

Low tech-high touch

We maintain that, as an example that is very relevant to us, the Chinyika phenomenon we witnessed in Zimbabwe (see Chapter 1) is a "low tech-high touch" version of the same network information economy as what we see in high-tech Silicon Valley. Economic and social history, as such, is cyclical as well as linear, non-linear as well as progressive. Both American and Zimbabwean versions, ideally and ultimately in combination, hold out the possibility of reversing two trends, for Benkler: concentration and commercialization.

In the process, we would be revisiting the pre-industrial old as well as proclaiming the post-industrial, and ultimately, altogether and necessarily between them, advancing the "alter-modern" case. In other words, America cannot fully advance in this networked informational sense, economically and socially, unless Zimbabwe does, as it were. In an alter-modern world of community activation, modern needs traditional and vice versa.

What Benkler, as we ourselves, are describing is not an exercise in utopianism. It is a practical possibility that directly results from our alternate economic understanding of "high-tech" information technology and "high-touch" culture and spirituality as objects of production. It flows from a new-old means of producing and exchanging information and culture placed in the hands of hundreds of thousands, and eventually millions, of people in adjacent villages, on the one hand, and in our "global village", on the other: trying to give meaning to their lives as social and cultural as well as economic and technological beings.

Commons based peer production

Free software then, as per Linux, like rural food security as per Chinyika, offers a glimpse at a basic and radical challenge. Both suggest that the networked environment makes possible a new modality of both organizing production and indeed, in this case here, community activation: radically decentralized, collaborative and non-proprietary based on sharing resources and outputs amongst widely distributed, loosely connected individuals, and indeed families, who cooperate with each other without relying either on market signals or managerial commands. This is what Benkler calls "commons-based peer production", whether for him globally, or for us, locally and communally.

Free open-source software

The story of Chinyika in Zimbabwe, started in the new millennium, instigated by Muchineripi and Kada, continues to unfold, through local-global Zimbabwean internet service provider Econet, duly activating rural communities in that light (see volume 3 on *Institutionalised Research*). The story of free software began in America 20 years before then, in 1984, when Richard Stallman started work on a project of building a non-proprietary operating system which he called GNU. Stallman, then at MIT, operated out of political conviction, whereas Muchineripi, and Kada, through BTD, operated out of human conviction: *Uri Munhu Here.* Stallman wanted a world in which software enabled people to use information freely; Muchineripi and Kada wanted a world in which their people respected their own culture, while being open to others, and thereby had food to eat.

These freedoms to share and make your own software, and foodstuffs, respectively, are fundamentally incompatible with a model of production that relied on property rights and markets. In that respect, free software was at the more immaterial end of production, whereas agricultural produce is relatively – only relatively – more at the material end.

The next major step came in the "north" when a person with a more practical, rather than prophetic, approach to his work began developing one central component of the operating system – the kernel. Linus Torvalds began sharing the early implementations of his kernel, called Linux, with others, under GPL. These ultimately 60,000 others then modified, added, contributed and shared among themselves these pieces of the operating system. Building on top of Stallman's foundation, Torvalds crystallized a model of production that was fundamentally different from those that preceded it. Moreover, such a model was not restricted to open source software.

The fate of the commons in a connected world

Commons and layers

For Bankler's fellow Harvard law professor Lawrence Lessig (Lessig, 2001), then, his focus is on the creativity and innovation that marked the early internet, but now extending beyond it, to the commons. This is the freedom that fuelled, for him, the greatest technological revolution that America has seen since the Industrial Revolution. While at the outset this seems very far removed from Zimbabwe and the world of Chinyika, as we have seen that is not entirely the case. Prior to his most recent appointment at Harvard, Lessig was a professor of law at Stanford Law School, where he founded the Center for Internet and Society, and at the University of Chicago. Lessig then turned to wireless communications.

Commons wireless

Early radio programming was different from today's. Indeed, there was no such thing as commercial radio. Radio at its start, in fact, looked a lot like the internet to begin with. Broadcasters on early radio included a wide range of noncommercial, religious and educational services. Commercial radio was just a fraction of the total. Around the early 1980s in fact, the rules governing the broadcast spectrum became an obsession with a retired West

Point officer in the US, David Hughes. Hughes had begun online community life in Colorado by setting up one of the first on-line bulletin boards in the nation. Though his work was technical, his motivation was communal:

> My work with radio has been based upon how you reach the smallest communities, and across community. Not just to it, but within it . . . It's always been to the end of the highest level of connectivity at the lowest cost for every community on the face of the globe.

Hughes began to push free access to spectrum. His work was designed to demonstrate how open spectrum could connect communities much more cheaply. At the core of his plan was a technology for sharing spectrum rather than allocating it – in other words, a plan for making the physical layer of the spectrum *free* by treating it as if it were a commons, a site for community activation. Hughes worked for a while with Federal Communications Commission's (FCC) technical adviser, Dewayne Hendricks. Hendricks had the idea to go elsewhere than the US to explore new ways to use the spectrum. The Kingdom of Tonga was receptive, and Hendricks proceeded to build a system to deliver high-speed internet access for all citizens in Tonga. And he has not stopped there. Encouraged by the FCC's push to develop internet infrastructure in Native American tribal lands, he then began a program to give Native American tribes access to free spectrum. So what overall lessons are there to be learned?

Conclusion

Towards a third social model

Complex modern societies, for Benkler as for Lessig, have developed in the context of mass media and an industrial information economy. Our prevailing theories of growth, whether in America, Zimbabwe or Nigeria, and innovation, are based on such industrial, as opposed to pre- or post-industrial models. Our theories about how effective communication in complex societies is achieved centre on market-based, proprietary approaches with a professional commercial core, and a dispersed, relatively passive periphery. To that extent, in Zimbabwe still, an Anglo-American would be considered core and a Chinyika peripheral, in the same way that in Nigeria a Unilever is core and a Paxherbals peripheral. For us, though, core and periphery are reversed, and to that extent innovation-driven institutionalized research, as we shall see, builds on prior community activation.

Something radically new, then, and also old, has started to happen. This rise of peer production is neither mysterious nor fickle when viewed through this lens, harking back, for us also, to the pre-modern. The pooling of human creativity, communication and storage enables non-market motivations and relations to play a much larger role in the institutionalized production of the information environment than it has been able to for decades, perhaps for as long as a century and a half, in the industrialized world. Yet in rural Zimbabwe and Nigeria, in Chinyika and Paxherbals at least, the agricultural commons is alive and well. How specifically might such apply to your own duly networked community activation?

Communication as basic human existence

Communication, in fact, is the basic unit, for Benkler, of social existence. Culture and knowledge, broadly conceived, form the basic frame of reference through which we come to understand ourselves and others in the "alter-modern" world, that combines pre- and post-industrial modalities. Independently, moreover, in the context of an innovation- and information-centric urban and rural economy, the basic components of human development also depend on such and how we disseminate its implementation.

From him then the emergence of a substantial role for non-proprietary production offers discrete strategies to improve human development, locally and globally. Productivity in the information economy, indigenously and exogenously, thereby extending community activation through such institutionalized research, can be sustained without the kinds of exclusivity that have made it difficult for knowledge and information to diffuse beyond the circles of the wealthiest nations and urban elites within the less wealthy. From the perspective of individual and communal autonomy, the emergence and thereafter institutional navigation of the networked information economy allows us to do more for and by ourselves, thereby allowing us to provide and explore many more diverse avenues of learning and speaking than we could achieve by ourselves or in association solely with others who share long-term string ties.

Towards a significant inflection point

We can remove some of the transactional barriers to material opportunity and improve the state of human development, locally, as per Chinyika or Paxherbals, globally, as per Linux, and ideally combine them both. Perhaps these changes, for Benkler (Benkler, 2011) as for Lessig, will be the foundation of a true transformation towards more co-creative and egalitarian societies. Perhaps they will merely improve human life in well-defined but smaller ways along each of these dimensions. That alone, for them as for us, is more than enough to justify an embrace of the networked information economy, north and south, east and west, by anyone who values human welfare, development and freedom. That is what community activation indeed means in this specific context.

More specifically then, and in conclusion, value provides the commons laden purpose; is sourced through peer to peer relationships in a community; builds on the culture through open source connectivity; resulting in a wealth of communal and institutional networks, culminating in an information society. We now turn from "north" to "west", from navigation to *effect*, albeit retaining the "southern" connection with *grounding* in *community activation,* duly aligned with an awakening of integral consciousness and institutionalized research.

References

Benkler, Y. (2006) *The Wealth of Networks: How Social Production Transforms Markets and Freedom.* London: Yale University Press.

Benkler, Y. (2011) *The Penguin and the Leviathan: How Cooperation Triumphs over Self-Interest.* New York: Crown Publishers.

Lessig, L. (2001) *The Future of Ideas: The Fate of the Commons in a Connected World.* New York: Vintage Books.

Part IV

Western communal effect

Build community, self-sufficiency, mutual development

10 Community building

An enterprise perspective on community activation

Summary of chapter:

1   socio-economic exchange then providing the value base to a community;
2   building on community/organizational culture via justice and reconciliation;
3   social business as the means of micro enterprise/macro economic navigation;
4   making a powerful effect through work- or community-based democracy;
5   finally turning markets, marketing, communications into community building.

Introduction: effecting a southern perspective on enterprise

Marketing, markets and communication to community building

So far we have focused on "southern" grounding, "eastern" emergence and awakening, and "northern" navigation and institutionalization, in relation to community activation, albeit that our overall emphasis is on grounding and origination. That said we now turn to "western" effect, first enterprise-wise, second economically, and finally in terms of embodying integral development.

We begin here with the effective transformation of the well known function of marketing into *community building* so that it resonates with community activation, as illustrated in Figure 10.1.

A keynote of our transpersonal and collective orientation, as such, is a correlation between the personal (self), the organizational (enterprise) and above all the communal (societal) (Table 10.1).

TENETS LG3/LE 3/LT 3/LF 3
Build Up Social Capital
Cultural, Political and Economic Commonwealth
Community Animation
Social Business

TENETS LG 4/LE 4/LT 4/ LF4	CORE TENET LG/LE/LT LF	TENETS LG 2/LE 2/LT2/ LF2
Community Ownership	*Community*	*Add Natural Value*
Great Work of Nature	*Activation/*	*Heal the Earth*
Action Research	**Secure Livelihood**	*People's Selfdevelopment*
Workplace Democracy	**Permaculture**	*Justice and Reconciliation*

Combine Action & Knowledge
Community Building
Lessem Schieffer, Yunus, Koopman

TENETS LG1/LE 1/LN1/LF1
Underlying Ubuntu
Pursue Earth Justice
Vivencia
Socio-Economic Exchange

Figure 10.1 Relational community activation: effective tenets.

Marketing in fact, as a "north-western", distinctly depersonalized, organizational function is taught on hundreds, if not thousands, of MBA and business studies programmes around the world. In depersonalized isolation, though, it is cut off from a natural or human community, which, in this "southern" instance, we align with natural and communal reciprocity.

Table 10.1 Community activation: enterprise perspective

From impersonal marketing to transpersonal community building reconnecting the southern vital functions of self, organization and society

Self: *communication*	Organization: *marketing*	Society: *markets*

Community building

Marketing to community building via social business

From an evolutionary perspective, in fact, marketing emerged out of primal (for Polanyi substantive) forces of what might be termed social and economic exchange, with which "southerners" are intimately familiar, rooted in physical nature and human community, reaching back millennia. It was only when salesmanship took hold as a specific business activity, alongside the notion that "the customer is king", that such social as well as economic exchange was supplanted by an individualized form of business and economic activity. That was further reinforced by the emergence of a somewhat depersonalized marketing management as a business function, as opposed to a public, civic or environmentally based one.

The subsequent development of relationships marketing, as well as, to some extent, service management, served to remind us of the originally communal and natural scope of physical and human exchange, which you revisit, in effect, in the course of community activation. In transforming marketing into community building, we are revisiting those communal and natural grounds, building upon ecology and anthropology, albeit now in twenty-first-century guise. Such a community building function, as opposed to marketing, is equally applicable to the public, civic and animate as it is to the private enterprise.

Southern ubuntu: I am because you are

Underlying such in "southern" African guise, as we saw in Chapter 1, is ubuntu: "I am because you are". The South African Peace Nobel Laureate Bishop Desmond Tutu (Tutu, 2002) provides us with an intimate perspective into ubuntu in the prelude of his acclaimed book, *No Future without Forgiveness.* Tutu asserts:

> When we want to give high praise to someone . . . we say Yu, u nobuntu: a person is a person through other persons. I am human because I belong. I participate, I share. In short, and in the words of our South African colleague and ex Member of Parliament Mfuniselwa Benghu (2), Ubuntu is an "African fundamental life philosophy, often considered the primary foundation of the African social-giving ethos".

In the following, we will guide you through the full GENE of community building, grounded most specifically here in *reciprocity and exchange*, emerging through *justice and reconciliation*, navigating via *social business* ultimately effected via *workplace democracy* (workplace combined with democracy), albeit retaining its primary connection with activating community.

Southern grounding: reciprocity and exchange

Hunter-gatherer antecedents of markets, marketing and communication

Oikos (Lessem, 1989) is the ancient Greek term for household, house or even family. At this late dawn of history, a village society had emerged in which life seemed to be unified by a communal disposition towards work, its products, as well as the exchange of such, within and between one community and another. The primal roots of business, of enterprise and of management, are therefore to be found in such gathering rather than in hunting. Not surprisingly, as we have said, the modern term "economics" derives from the Greek term "oikos", a sense of place, and also the source of "ecology".

In fact, it was not until the seventeenth and eighteenth centuries, Adam Smith's *Wealth of Nations* appearing in 1776, that economics and enterprise were transformed, and gradually lost their homely connection, one that the "social entrepreneur" today may be seeking to rediscover. The business entrepreneur, then, and the derivative business enterprise, visibly evolved from hunting origins. Such an entrepreneurial tradition has lived on since, most evidently in "western" guise, and has gained force recently, in both developed and transitional societies. Thus the original hunting image, stretching back to Neolithic times, retains much of its primal force and identity.

The gatherer's role and evolution towards social business

The communal, ecological tradition, on the other hand, has undergone an ironic transformation. The gatherer has been thrust out of classical economics, despite the original "oikos". It reappears in the nineteenth century in Marxian guise. By this point, the gatherer is sitting outside and in opposition to business. In the twentieth century this results in the Russian and Chinese revolution, and now of course we have, in these two countries, a kind of backlash. Whereas then in the twentieth century the stage was set for a clash between "capitalism" and "socialism", both of which by-passed the "gatherer", in the twenty-first century capitalism has reasserted itself, and again the gatherer is left out in the cold. What we are doing here is to bring it back into the picture. We do so in newly "southern" communal guise. In fact, Ghana's statesman-philosopher, Kwame Nkrumah (Nkrumah, 1970), referred to Aristotle in his *Consciencism*: "Aristotle's humanism was a co-operative one, in which each man, perceiving a different aspect of the truth, contributed to the common whole".

Exchange and reciprocity

Actually, such principles of social and economic exchange as well as of reciprocity are alive and well in parts of Africa today. Susanne Gutierrez (1986) pointed out in her research in the 1980s on the market women of Nigeria:

> There is a clear reflection of European commercial and philosophical influences – in the emerging impersonal, formal and specialised attitude – in today's African institutions. In the marketplace, however, women are able to transcend these influences and bring to their daily lives the historical African sense of family and community. Regardless of the sophistication of the surrounding community, no matter how urbanised and industrialised it may become, the market-place prevails as a centre of trade and communication, whether the traders are dealing in cement, tomatoes, or television sets.

In fact, the cultural anthropologists Ellis and Ter Haar (2004) have more recently given us a new perspective on money and markets in an African context:

> Throughout West Africa, the morality of exchange has been associated with the markets. West African markets are real meeting places, not just virtual or technical places of exchange. Some are regulated by sophisticated conventions on the pricing and sale of goods. They are rather like the "agora" of the ancient Greeks, places to meet friends and talk as well as to do business; they are places of fundamental social importance.

Southern emergence: healing and reconciliation

From exchange to reconciliation

The communal grounding in economic and social exchange is as old as the hills. The reformation that has taken place, in recent years, most poignantly so in South Africa, is the turning of such exchange and reciprocity, at a societal level, into healing and reconciliation, while in Nigeria via Paxherbals (see Chapter 2) it has happened at a community-enterprise level. In fact, the South African academic theologian John De Gruchy, in the context of

South Africa's "Truth and Reconciliation Commission", in his book on *Reconciliation – Restoring Justice* (De Gruchy, 2000), has pointed out that:

> The Greek words translated in the New Testament by "reconciliation" or "reconcile" are compounds of the Greek "to exchange", and this in turn is derived from the Greek word meaning "the other". The words thus carry with them the sense of exchanging places with "the other" and therefore being in solidarity with rather than against such "another".

Covenanting together to restore justice

Nelson Mandela declared in his inaugural speech to the South African public in May 1994 (Mandela, 1994a):

> We enter a covenant that we shall build a society in which all South Africans, both black and white, will be able to walk, without any fear in their hearts, assured of their inalienable right to human dignity – a rainbow nation at peace with itself and the world.

Such reconciliation is about building bridges, about allowing conflicting stories to interact in ways that evoke respect, about building relationships including economic ones, and helping restructure power relations. This means that we have to go beyond a political, social or economic agreement to co-exist across those rivers that divide, and find ways to engender common endeavour, including that between producer and consumer. A covenantal relationship, in other words, goes further than a social or business contract because it is concerned about animate, civic, public reconciliation rather than mere private or commercial reconciliation, in financial and economic terms. It involves building up "equity", not only in a financial and economic sense but also in a social and communal one (Table 10.2).

Market to restorative economics

Bishop Desmond Tutu (Tutu, 2002), in the latter part of the nineties, built upon the notion of "restorative" justice. He contrasts it with market economics, also building upon notions of exchange and reciprocity, for a South African process of Reconstruction and Development (RDP):

> In South Africa today, the resources of the state have to be deployed imaginatively, wisely, efficiently and equitably, to facilitate the reconstruction process in a manner which best brings relief and hope to the widest sections of the community, developing for the benefit of the

Table 10.2 CARE as community building

Communal activation: community building southern relational effect communication, markets and marketing
• *Communal attributes*: grounding – livelihood, healing, truth quest; emergence – permaculture, vitality of place, disclosing new worlds; navigation – participatory, study circles, networks; effect – *community building*, self-sufficiency, mutual advantage. • *Integrator role*: community steward, e.g. *Albert Koopman*, Cashbuild SA. • *Communal function*: transforming individual communications, corporate marketing and societally based markets. • *Grounded in value*: *socio-economic exchange provide*s the value base; is sourced through *in* a community; builds on the culture through *justice and reconciliation*; *social business* becomes the means of micro enterprise/ macro economic navigation; at best a powerful contribution to *work based democracy*; at their worst nepotism prevails.

entire nation the latent human potential and resources of every person who has directly or indirectly been burdened with the heritage of the shame and the pain of the country's racist past . . . to take into account the competing claims on resources, with regard to the "untold suffering" of individuals.

In our terms here, Tutu specifically and South Africa generally mirror the world at large. And in terms of reconciliation means also that social and economic exchange is the communal base for markets and for justice. Indeed, a further journeying is required, for every enterprise to evolve through its community, as well as for every community to evolve through its business. To bring such a concept of community and enterprise to light, we turn from "southern" grounding (reciprocity and exchange) and emergence (justice and reconciliation) to navigation (social business). As such we turn to Grameen and to Yunus, in Bangladesh.

Southern navigation: social business

Introducing social business

Mohammad Yunus (2008) has by now gained international renown, including the award of the Nobel Peace Prize, for his work on micro lending in Bangladesh (which we locate here in the "south"), through the Grameen Bank. We now turn to his latest work (in the next chapter we pursue his overall economic effect in Bangladesh more fully), following on from where De Gruchy, Mandela and Tutu in South Africa have left off, in *Creating a World without Poverty*. Indeed, we shall review his overall economic approach, further, in the next chapter. Mainstream free-market theory, which South Africa, for example, was obliged to conform to in the 1990s, suffers, for Yunus, overall, from a "conceptualization failure", a failure to capture the essence of what it is to be human.

Profit-maximizing versus social business

By insisting that all businesses must be profit-maximizing (PMB), we have ignored the multi-dimensionality of human beings and, as a result, business remains incapable of addressing many of our most pressing social problems. A "social business", for Yunus then, is not a charity. It concentrates on creating products and services that create benefits for a community, and recovers its costs in the process, for example through:

- providing nutritious foods to poor and underfed children;
- designing and marketing affordable medical care for the poor;
- developing renewable energy systems at a price they can afford;
- recycling garbage, sewage and other waste products in poor and politically powerless neighbourhoods.

Once the social- and objective-driven project overcomes the gravitational force of financial dependence, it is ready for a space flight. As the social business grows, so do the benefits it provides to society. Cashbuild in South Africa is a case in point.

Southern transformative effect: workplace democracy

Mutual development

The Cashbuild case is unique in South Africa to this day. With Albert Koopman at the helm of this provider of building supplies in the rural areas of the country, the company was not only ultimately transformed into a workplace democracy but became distinctively profitable, socially as well as economically. Moreover, this initially took place in apartheid South Africa, where the conditions for such social and economic reconciliation could not have been worse. How then did Koopman manage such an ultimately successful process of mutual development, between community and society, including conflict resolution, duly incorporating the advance of human rights with such a profitable enterprise? Let Koopman tell his own story (Koopman, 1991).

Cashbuild was started as a wholesaler in 1978 and became a very successful business in a short space of time. Situated predominantly in the rural areas of South Africa and focusing on the black housing market, our staff consisted of 84% black, 13% white and 3% Indian. However by mid 1982, with 12 outlets, profits started sliding. Everything "northern" was in place – systems, procedures, technology, combined with a booming market – but something was going wrong and I did not know enough about the south, at that point, to recognise where to start looking.

Introducing our care philosophy

I was therefore forced to seek a way in which we could spell out and determine our objective common interest in the production of commodities – customer service (southern) – to replace capital's pure interest in increasing profits (western). Lots of meetings, small group activities, discussion groups and open two-way communications had to form as much of the way we ran our business as did the work itself. Everything had to be focussed upon the common interest of creating wealth and fostering an understanding amongst workers that the correct management of capital benefits the organization as a whole.

This correct management, in turn, could only occur if the worker was democratically involved in contributing towards the overall success of

Table 10.3 The advent of Venturecomm

Competitive versus communal	
Individual competitive	*Group communal*
Profit for me is derived from self-interest	Profit to me is a vote of confidence my society gives me for service rendered to that society
I am actually exclusive from my fellow man	I am mutually inclusive
I prefer to be a self-actualised person	I prefer to be a social man
The more I have, the more I am	I am, therefore I share and give
I demand productivity from people	I prefer to create a climate in which people will be willingly more productive
I am actually an aggressive kind of person	I am actually a receptive kind of a person
I look you in the eye and challenge you	I bow my head and show my respect
My concern is for production	My concern is for people

the organization. I visualised that in this manner so-called capitalist exploitation (of the "southern" community) would no longer be able to exist. Exploitative capitalism demands quotas, productivity and quality, all as part of a commodity outlook on life. People remain part of the production-distribution-consumption process without their spiritual work or social ethos being recognized. The protagonists of class-consciousness, meanwhile, became a rallying point in the name of social justice, without actually giving expression to the human face. We promptly decided at Cashbuild to pursue our own course. We needed a social form that could accommodate the freedom to be enterprising, as well as harnessing the spiritual consciousness of all our employees. "Our CARE structures, as representatively democratic, were still separating management and worker".

What they were crying out for was for participatory democracy, thereby integrating their economic and social selves, so as to relieve labour power of its commodity character. It dawned upon me as a result that:

- No one can demand productivity from anyone, but I can create a climate within which social man is willingly productive.
- I cannot manage people, only things, but I can create a climate within which people take responsibility and manage themselves.
- One cannot demand quality from people, but I can create conditions at work through which quality work is a product of pride in workmanship.

A convention of some 200 workers was held and the ground rules were established:

- Respect human dignity and individual freedom of speech.
- Allow everyone to have access to company results and performance standards.
- Give everyone a role in developing company policy.
- Improve the quality of life of all employees outside the work sphere through active community involvement.

Towards workplace democracy

I could now see that if I recognised and restored the dignity and pride of the workforce I could achieve a new human spirit that would drive the enterprise for the betterment of all.

It was proposed that a governing body of five people be constituted to each outlet – the VENTURECOMM – with each person being democratically elected to hold a portfolio, save for the manager who was appointed to the operations portfolio, based on his or her expertise. This portfolio was concerned with the "hard" variables whereas the safety, labour, merchandise and quality of work-life portfolios were the "soft" ones.

Moreover, each of these managers was continually assessed by lower levels in the hierarchy. In fact, this Cashbuild VENTURECOMMM system was socialistic in that it instated social justice and offered security against destitution. It was likewise capitalistic to the extent that individual expression was given its due reward, and group development its due recognition. Our system thus gave expression to the work ethic and also to the enterprising spirit of people.

Conclusion: towards community building

Cashbuild in today's South Africa is still a thriving commercial business, with a well-developed marketing model, but, with Koopman and his protégé Haumant having long gone, it is no longer, in Yunus' terms, a "social business". The fate of Cashbuild is replicated across the world's stage. Because the "western" model of free market capitalism, economically, and the model of the shareholder controlled, market oriented corporation, commercially, is so dominant, community building on a sustainable basis is curtailed. Instead, and relationally overall, socio-economic exchange provides the value base, sourced through and in a community; builds further on the community/organizational culture through justice and reconciliation; social business becomes the means of micro enterprise and macro economic navigation; at best making a powerful contribution through work or community based democracy.

The question then ultimately is, herein, in what respect have you served to bring about, or enhance, the integral effect of community activation?

We now turn from "southern" community building, from an enterprise perspective, to "south-eastern" self-sufficiency, from an economic perspective, altogether concerned with community activation, this time more fully illustrated by Grameen in Bangladesh.

References

Bhengu, M. (2015) *Amazulu: Ancient Egyptian Origin*. Durban, South Africa: Mepho Publishers.

De Gruchy, J. (2000) *Reconciliation – Restoring Justice*. Canterbury, UK: SCM Press.

Ellis, S and Ter Haar, G. (2004) *Worlds of Power*. Johannesburg, South Africa: Wits University Press.

Gutierrez, S. (1986) *Market Women of Nigeria*. PhD Thesis. London: City University Business School.

Koopman, A. (1991) *Transcultural Management*. Chichester, UK: Wiley-Blackwell.

Lessem, R. (1989) *Global Management Principles*. Hillsdale, NJ: Prentice Hall.

Mandela, N. (1994a) Inaugural speech. www.bet.com/news/global/2013/12/05/transcript-nelson-mandela-s-1994-inauguration-speech.html (accessed October 2016).

Mandela, N. (1994b) *Long Walk to Freedom*. Grand Rapids, MI: Abacus.

Nkrumah, K. (1970) *Consciencism*. New York: Monthly Review Press.

Tutu, D. (2002) *No Future Without Forgiveness*. New York: Doubleday.

Yunus, M. (2008) *Creating a World without Poverty*. New York: Public Affairs.

11 Self-sufficiency

An economic perspective on community activation

Summary of chapter:

1 begin with community providing the value base;
2 starting the economic engine at the rear;
3 building up towards creating a world without poverty;
4 such community building results in the proliferation of social business;
5 ultimately establishing self-sufficiency in the society as a whole.

Introduction: Grameen – a bank for the poor

Rooted in community life: Grameen "village"

In turning marketing into community building we have recast enterprise, from a "southern" relational perspective, into a new guise, one that constitutes the culminating enterprise effect of community activation. How might the same arise, serving if you like to renew and extend such community building within the economy at large, and to what extent, through your own community activation, are you engaged with such? Grameen in Bangladesh, as we shall now see, is a good "south-eastern" case in point, in this case focused, effectively and transformatively, on building up self-sufficiency, widely and developmentally.

Grameen (which means "village" in Bengali) has provided, since the 1980s, a significant application of the principle of self-sufficiency within an emergent developmental economy. It is a remarkable example, spearheaded by Muhammad Yunus (Yunus, 1999) as we initially saw in the previous chapter, of a community-based economic alternative emerging out of one of the most poverty stricken countries on earth, thereby creating an entire alternative, self-sufficient economic system. Figure 11.1 shows the effective tenets to renewed community activation.

Grameen, moreover, is deeply rooted in "nature and community", as Yunus' journey started out in agriculturally based rural Bangladesh. Grameen additionally draws on the Bangladeshi culture and spirit of craftsmanship and self-sufficiency, thereby building up a subsistence economy in that country. Yunus, himself an American educated, thereafter renegade economist, challenged the conventional "western" wisdom, whereby "greed" or Adam Smith's "self interest" is the core driver of the entrepreneur and enterprise, and replaces it with social goals as a more powerful, and for him equally pervasive, motivational force. Grameen (meaning: rural, village) builds in all its facets *on* community, is embedded *in* community and is also owned *by* the community, with about 90 per cent of its shares owned by its borrowers.

For Grameen's employees, now amounting to over 13,000, Yunus was not just a CEO; much more, he was a teacher. Altogether, Grameen also represents a new emergent economic paradigm. On a microeconomic level, Yunus, based on the Grameen experience, developed the concept of a social business. On a macroeconomic level, Grameen, from the grassroots, has

TENETS NG3/NE 3/NT 3/NF3
Combining Nature, Spirit, Science, Economy
Socially Embedded Institutions
Flexible Framework
<u>*Create a World without Poverty*</u>

TENETS NG 4/NE 4/NT 4 NF4	CORE TENET LG/LE/NT/ NF	TENETS NG 2/NE 2/NT 2/ NF2
Communitalism	*Community*	*Fusing Work and Prayer*
Trade and Accumulation	*Activation/*	*Communal Relationships*
Collective Learning	**Heal Community**	*Informal Character*
<u>*Actualize Social Business*</u>	**Vitality of Place**	<u>*Start Economic Engine at Rear*</u>
	Study Circles	
	<u>**Selfsufficiency**</u>	

TENETS NG1/NE 1/NT1/NF1
Nature Power
Value Base
Genuine Interest
<u>*Begin with Community*</u>

Figure 11.1 Renewed community activation: effective tenets.

contributed to building a new Bangladeshi economy, by branching out in evermore economic sectors: from banking to telecommunications, from fishery to clothing and textiles, from healthcare to housing, thereby effectively activating community economically. It is a case that demonstrates that for each country to economically fully flourish, poverty in all its variations needs to be addressed. Table 11.1 shows the "eastern" renewal effect in respect of Grameen. In what way then is your community activation aligned with this?

Common ownership

Grameen came into existence with the following objectives:

- extend banking facilities to poor people;
- eliminate the exploitation of the poor by money lenders;
- create opportunities for self-employment for the multitude;
- bring the disadvantaged, mostly women from the poorest households, into the economic fold in an organizational format they can manage for themselves;
- reverse the age-old vicious circle of "low income, low saving, low investment".

Today, Grameen Bank is owned by the rural poor whom it serves. Borrowers of the bank own 90 per cent of its shares, while the remaining 10 per cent are owned by the government. What then was the overall philosophy that gave rise to it?

Table 11.1 CARE as self-sufficiency

Communal activation: self-sufficiency in a developmental economy eastern renewal effect the case of Grameen in Bangladesh
• *Communal attributes*: south – ubuntu, primal, communitalism; east – organic, embedded, solidarity; north – networks, study circles, participatory; west – community building, *self-sufficiency*, mutual aid.
• *Integrator role*: community steward, e.g. *Muhammad Yunus*, Grameen.
• *Communal function*: structured along *common ownership* lines.
• *Grounded in value*: *begin with community* (I am because you are) provides the value base; is sourced through *starting the economic engine at the rear*; builds up towards *creating a world without poverty*; at best such community building results in the proliferation of *social business*; at their worst parochial rivalries prevail.

Starting the economic engine at the rear

Focused on the welfare of stakeholders

In his youth, Yunus, like many Bengalis of his generation, was influenced by Marxist economics, but, as an advocate of an "open society", he never liked such dogma (Lessem and Schieffer, 2010). He was never an Islamist, but neither was he willing to give up his culture, his prayers, or respect for the Prophet. Without the human side, he felt, economics was just as hard and dry as a stone. In fact, he departed from his singular role as an economics academic in Bangladesh for that very reason.

In the US, where he studied for his doctorate in conventional economics, he saw how the market liberates the individual and allows people to be free to make personal choices. But the biggest drawback was that the market always pushes things onto the side of the individual and the powerful. So Yunus needed to find a way in which the poor could use the market system to their advantage. Over time, then, Grameen was to become a commonly held bank, one through which its members gained personal wealth in order to acquire water pumps, latrines, housing, schools, health services and so on. What then is your equivalent?

Grameen has always tried to run at a profit, to cover costs, to protect itself from future shocks and to carry on its expansion, but its overall concerns were and are focused on the welfare of all its stakeholders – the bank's borrowers and employees being also its shareholders – not on immediate return on the investment dollar.

Poverty is created by the structures of society

According to Yunus, "Poverty is not created by the poor . . . it is created by the structures of society. Change the structures, as Grameen has done, and you will see the poor changing their lives". Yunus argues that somehow we have persuaded ourselves that the capitalist economy, ever more so today, must be fuelled by greed. This has become a self-fulfilling prophecy. He firmly believes that greed is not the only fuel for free enterprise and that social goals can replace greed as a powerful motivational force.

What then constitutes true economic development? For Yunus, changing the quality of life of the bottom 25 per cent of the population, not an overall rise in per capita income, is the essence of such development. Not only do the different economic layers of society, he argues, move at different speeds but they do not even move in the same direction unless extreme care is taken along the way. Worse still, if the engines of social groups at the tail-end are not turned on, not only may they not be pulled by the engines at the front, they may start sliding backwards, independently from the rest of society, and to the detriment of everyone involved, including the better off.

Micro-credit, the business that Grameen was primarily in, starts up the economic engine at the rear end of the train by starting up the engine in each passenger in that usually decaying and putrid carriage. This cannot reduce the speed of the train, it can only increase it, which most of today's so-called development projects fail to do. Micro-credit, for Yunus, ignites the tiny economic engines of the rejected underclass of society, by providing them with the means of securing their own subsistence. How then did Grameen start out in its own illustrious life?

Starting with community

Grameen made a small start in 1976, with the kind of participatory action research we saw in Chapter 7. It invited an NGO, the Center for Mass Education in Science, to organize life-oriented education in a village near Dhaka, the capital of Bangladesh. After one year 1,600 adult learners were reached in 25 centres, each having 45 learners. These were the early seeds, sown, for what was to become a bank, and, thereafter, the provider of a multifaceted physical, social and economic infrastructure for the poor people of Bangladesh.

Continuing with nature

The Bangladeshi famine in the late seventies, occurring soon after Yunus had initiated the action research project, led him to focus all his efforts on farming, which is where the story of the development of the bank as an institution began. Bangladesh, a territory of 35 million acres and one of the most densely populated in the world, needed to increase its food production. Specialists estimated that the existing crop yields amounted to only 16 per cent of farm potential. Yunus decided he should help the neighbouring villagers of Jobra to grow more food. He and his students offered their services to help plant high-yielding rice. In the winter of 1975, moreover, his attention fell to solving the problem of irrigation to raise an extra winter crop.

Questioning finance

Realizing though that his work with farmers failed to reach the most destitute, Yunus turned his mind to the problem of the landless, assetless people with no ready made access to the commons. Their condition of utter destitution made them fighters, and not being tied to the land, they were more mobile, more open to ideas, and more enterprising than the farmers.

Sufia Begum's story, for example, made him sit up. Yunus could not believe that a woman, crafting bamboo chairs, could suffer a life of bonded labour – bonded to her moneylender – because she was unable to find the 20 cents a day to fund her business. So he drove to the local branch of the Janata Bank, a government institution and one of the biggest in the country, to negotiate a loan on Sufia's behalf. He failed utterly to secure any kind of loan without collateral. So he ended up advancing the money himself, but that was no kind of long-term solution. Meanwhile Yunus was in the process of discovering, as he put it, "the world's basic banking principle – the more you have the more you get; if you don't have it, you don't get it". Perhaps unwittingly, banks had designated a class of people as "not creditworthy". Out of desperation, Yunus was led to question the most basic banking premise, that of collateral.

Its shareholders are its borrowers

Grameen then looked at conventional banks and turned everything upside down. Conventional banks ask their clients to come to their office. An office is a terrifying place for the poor and illiterate. So they decided to go to the clients. The entire Grameen system is based on that principle.

In a commercial bank, bankers are only answerable to their shareholders, to maximize the bank's profits, subject to limits set by governments and regulators. Grameen too is answerable to shareholders. With the exception of the about 10 per cent of stock owned by government, its shareholders are its borrowers. The bank seeks a high return for its shareholders, but this may be in the form of improved housing and standard of living. In Grameen then, people's needs and lives are not a sideline, it is what comes first and foremost. All the rest is merely a means to advance its goals of transforming the lives of borrowers and their dependants.

Success therefore is not measured by bad debt figures or repayment rates – though such records need to be kept – but whether the lives of borrowers have become less miserable. Ultimately, Yunus would like all his borrowers to rise above the poverty line. Special housing loans, for example, have provided leak-proof homes for 425,000 families; while another 150,000 homes have been built from Grameen funded enterprises. "Grameen is thereby promoting social as well as economic change. It wants women, hitherto adjudged second-class citizens, to make decisions about their fate and their families".

Grameen: much more than a bank

Today, the Grameen Bank is much more than a bank in the conventional sense. This enlarged role can be traced back to its response to persistent flooding in Bangladesh. If a flood or a famine decimates a village and kills a borrower's crops or animals, Grameen will immediately and always lend the borrower new money to start up again. The old loan is converted into a very long-term loan, so that the borrower can pay it off very slowly. Bangladesh has so many natural disasters that often an area will be hit by several in the same year. Yet now Grameen is so much more than a financial institution.

Building a self-sufficient economy: Grameen bank to Grameenphone

Rebuilding the economy

While on the one hand Grameen had brought micro-credit onto a global stage, on the other, it increasingly reached out, within Bangladesh, into new sectors. Now that the commercial side of the Grameen Bank had proved itself and was actively changing people's lives, thereby providing an underlying basis for self-sufficiency, Yunus wanted to build on this success and expand into other areas. He thereby wanted to improve the quality of life of Grameen's borrowers, as well as that of the community in general. Specifically, he was looking towards market-oriented ways of improving the social infrastructure, which the government was not providing, or was providing inadequately. Thereby, Grameen virtually started to rebuild the Bangladeshi economy from the grassroots.

Providing housing and healthcare

Grameen has expanded the types of loans it makes available to borrowers to finance such quality of life items as water wells, flush toilets and housing. It is also creating self-financing enterprises that will cover its borrowers' health, retirement and education, as well as meet the needs of the community at large.

It is trying to make health care available to all its borrowers and to other villagers on a self-financing, cost-recovery basis, asking people to pay $3 per family per year as a health premium. So social infrastructure is indeed part of poverty alleviation. But good infrastructure, by itself, will not create wealth. It creates a required enabling environment in the war against poverty.

Clothing the nation

In Bangladesh there are about one million handloom weavers desperately looking for a market for their product. In 1993, Grameen created an independent, non-stock, not-for-profit company to do just that. It was called Grameen Uddog (Initiatives). The objective of the company was to link up the traditional handloom weavers with the export-oriented garment industry.

The weavers produced the cloth Grameen asked for, and, for Yunus, it was beautiful. They themselves took great pride in the export market. The name given to the fabric was "Grameen Check".

Fish farming: feeding the poor

Fish farming was Grameen's next port of call. As it had no experience, it enrolled staff on crash courses on how to farm fish. Grameen sent staff to China to learn about pond management and hatchery operations. Practical skills were developed through learning by doing. Eventually the large initial capital investment and the training of staff began to pay off. Grameen organized the poor around the ponds to become partners in business. They gave their labour, guarded the ponds against poaching and Grameen provided all the inputs, technology and management. Technology is an essential prerequisite for raising productivity, but unless Grameen directs who it is who will receive the increased production, it will end up – Yunus believes – in the hands of the rich.

Grameenphone: technology for the poor

The government of Bangladesh issued three cellular licences in 1996 to Grameen. On Independence Day, in March 1997, a service was launched, which promised to bring IT to all the people of Bangladesh, even the poorest. Grameen formed two independent companies, one for profit (Grameenphone), and the other not-for-profit (Grameen Telecom). The former is a consortium made up of four partners: Telenor of Norway (51 per cent), Grameen Telecom (35 per cent), Marubeni of Japan (9.5 per cent) and Gonophone Development Company (4.5 per cent). Grameenphone was the recipient of the licence. It was to serve all urban areas by building a nationwide network. Grameen Telecom was to buy bulk airtime from Grameenphone and retail it from Grameen borrowers in all the villages of Bangladesh. One Grameen borrower in each of the 68,000 villages was to become "the telephone lady". Thus the village would be connected to the world through a poor woman who uses the most modern communication system available to earn a better living for herself.

Conclusion: creating a world without poverty

Creating a level playing field for everyone

The real question for Yunus is not so much where he thinks we will be in the year 2050, but what world he would like to be in by then. When schoolchildren, 50 years hence, go with their teachers and tour the poverty museums, they will be horrified to see the misery and indignity of human beings. They will blame their forefathers for tolerating this inhuman condition and for allowing it to continue for a large part of the population until the early part of the twenty-first century.

Eliminating poverty from the world is a matter of will rather than the finding of ways and means. So how strong is your will in that respect? Charity only perpetuates poverty by taking the initiative away from the poor. But the real issue is creating a level playing field for everybody, giving every human being a fair and equal chance (Lessem and Schieffer, 2010). Such socially desired changes may not be attractive from the greed perspective. For Yunus, therefore, socially-consciousness-driven organizations are necessary. The state and civil society must provide the respective support and financial resources. For these organizations will need to continually devote their attention and R & D money to those areas of innovation, which will facilitate the development of social goals.

That is why Grameen was awarded the Nobel Peace Prize rather than the prize for economics.

Bangladesh as a living laboratory

Bangladesh, for Yunus writing in 2008 (Yunus, 2008), is a living laboratory, one of the world's poorest countries that is being transformed by innovative social and business thinking, about how to improve the economy of the commons. What is the parallel in your community and society? Since the mid 1980s then:

- The poverty rate in Bangladesh has fallen from 74 per cent (1974) to 40 per cent (2005).
- The country's rapid economic growth (6.7 per cent in 2006) has not been accompanied by growing inequality.
- Population growth has fallen sharply from 3 per cent in the 1970s to 1.5 per cent in 2000, driven by improvements in healthcare.
- The percentage of children completing the 5th grade has increased from 49 per cent in 1990 to 74 per cent in 2004; more girls now attend secondary schools than boys.
- Between 1980 and 2004, the Human Development Index increased by 45 per cent compared to 39 per cent in India.

As such, Grameen has begun with community providing the value base; thereby starting the economic engine at the rear; building up towards creating a world without poverty; at best such community building results in the proliferation of social business. What is the equivalent for you? We now turn, finally, from self-sufficiency to mutual development.

References

Lessem, R. and Schieffer, A. (2010) *Integral Economics: Releasing your Economic Genius*. Abingdon, UK: Routledge.

Yunus, M. (1999) *Banker for the Poor*. New York: Aurum.

Yunus, M. (2008) *Creating a World Without Poverty*. New York: Public Affairs.

12 Mutual development

Purveyors of the province

A mutual educational perspective on community activation

Summary of chapter:

1   soil, river, forest provide the value base;
2   enhanced through purveyors of the province as transformative educators;
3   building on such through a provincial diversity of socio-economic structures;
4   effected through powerful cultural, political, economic *zemstvo* (local government);
5   ultimately transforming education by pursuing mutual development.

Introduction: transformative education

Mutual development at a provincial level

In this fourth and final part of *effecting* community activation we have turned from transformative enterprise via the "southern" relational (community building) and a transformative approach to economics (self-sufficiency) via to the "eastern" path of renewal (Grameen), to embodying integral development on now the reasoned realization "north-western" path via provincial purveyors in nineteenth-century Russia (mutual development). Bear in mind overall though, because we are altogether concerned with community activation, collectively, we remain close to the communal and natural ground, albeit on three different paths (see Figure 12.1).

In alluding to Russia pursuing such mutual development, through primarily community activation, and secondarily awakening of consciousness, institutionalized research and now embodying integral development (Lessem, 2016), we have had to turn the clock back to locate such at a provincial level. For neither Russia specifically, nor indeed the Soviet Union

TENETS NE 3/SE 3/SN3/SV3
Discursive Community
Disclosing New Worlds
Open Source
Diversity of Socio-economic Structures

TENETS NE 4/SE 4/SN4 SV4	CORE TENET LG/LE/SN SV	TENETS NE2/ SE2/SN2 SV2
Individuation	Community	*Restorative Big Picture*
History Making	Activation/	*Cultivating Solidarity*
Wealth of Networks	**Truth Quest**	*Peer-to-Peer*
Provincial Zemstvo	**Fashioning Anew**	Purveyors of the Province
	Information Society	
	Pursuit of Mutual Development	

TENETS NE1/SE1/SN1/SV1
Direct Democracy
Virtuous Citizen
Natural & Social Commons
Soil, River and Forest

Figure 12.1 Reasoned community activation: effective tenets.

generally, have succeeded in pursuing such today as a whole. Both were too busy trying to catch up with the "west", as per Peter the Great in the eighteenth century or Lenin and then Stalin in the twentieth, all too often oppressing their own people in the process.

Should we raise the question of what all this has to do with our own community activation, the answer, as we shall see, is that Russia lost its way in the same way that so many communities and societies do, because there was no agency there, at the turn of the nineteenth century, to recognize and release its genius. As an individual, US-based Russian historian Catherine Evtuhov (Lessem *et al.*, 2014) is arguably such an agent, reflectively though not actively.

Table 12.1 shows the transformative educational effect of "north-western" realization.

The heart of the country

Professor Catherine Evtuhov, based at Georgetown University in Washington, DC, set out to uncover the nature and scope of a typical Russian province in the late nineteenth century, in the reform period after the emancipation of

Table 12.1 CARE as mutual development

Communal activation: mutual development transformative educational effect of north-western realization transformative educators as purveyors of the province
• *Communal attributes*: south – ubuntu, primal, communitalism; east – organic, vitality, solidarity; north – networks, study circles, participatory; west – community building, self-sufficiency, *mutual aid*. • *Integrator role*: community steward, e.g. *Alexander Gatsiskii – ethnographist*. • *Communal function*: pursuit of *mutual development*. • *Grounded in value*: *soil, river, forest* provides the value base; is sourced through *educators as purveyors of the province in* a community; builds on the culture through a provincial *diversity of socio-economic structures*; at best such community building makes for a powerful cultural, political and economic *zemstvo*; at their worst narrowly based national despotism prevails.

the serfs (Evtuhov, 2011). She chose Nizhnii Novgorod province, in the heart of Russia. Her intention was to uncover not only what is unique to a Russian province, the size of Belgium or Greece, but also what is generalizable to the nation as a whole. Moreover, she wanted to illustrate the nature and scope of such a local, or regional, Russian consciousness, lodged in a typical "province". In the process, as we shall see, she overturns the conventional wisdom on Russia's primarily agrarian heritage, and thereby intimates that there is something more integral than meets the conventional historical, military, political, economic eye.

Moreover, the last third of the nineteenth century, for her, was the "Age of the Congresses". Every action of the Nizhnii Novgorod's *zemstvo* (local government) had became inscribed in larger, national Russian efforts. Whilst the oldest and best known civic institutions remained the Free Economic Society and the Russian Technical Society, a plethora of ad hoc associations or regular meetings appeared "middle-up-down-across" in every profession and organization. A network of "invisible threads" linked the provinces to each other and to the nation as a whole. How was this achieved?

Transformative educators as purveyors of the province

Pivotal to all of this, for Evtuhov, were what she calls the "purveyors" of the province, which we have likened to transformative educators and researchers, not to mention also their powers as community activists, duly awakening integral consciousness. Their goal as such was to depict, describe, conceptualize, present and promote the province. The most prominent amongst these, for example, was Alexander Gatsiskii. Author of some 400 articles on local history, popular religion, archaeology, ethnography and statistics, he entered the national limelight in the 1970s as defender of the "provincial idea" the notion that Russia's provinces had a crucial role to play in national development.

Arguably, as community activists, and overall CARErs, you are also such "purveyors" of your province, so to speak, in some shape or form. How indeed do you see yourself as a transformative educator in that light?

Nature and economy

Fashioning the soil

We can think of the parameters of the interaction in the Nizhnii Novgorod region, according to Evtuhov, starting out with nature and community, in terms of the trinity of soil, forest and river. The soil could be seen as a natural-historical body, resulting from the collective influence of five underlying factors: the subsoil's climate, flora and fauna, geological age, and the relief of the locality.

Each of the above are *soil-fashioners*, representing an endless series of degrees, variations, peculiarities, altogether related to each other. The soil, in other words, lay at the intersection of a variety of apparently external factors; studying it, as researcher-and-educator, seriously required bringing into play insights from minerology, geology, chemistry, physics, meteorology, biology and geography. If it is possible to speak of a specific result of this many-layered, complex approach, it would be multiplicity and variability. We now turn from soil to forest.

Primordial, agricultural and industrial forest

Romantic poets like to talk of primordial forests. In Eurasia, natural scientists and geographers have classified five distinct natural "belts" related to such, moving from north to south: tundra, forest, forest-steppe, steppe and desert, Nizhnii Novgorod itself falling between forest and steppe. Forests, however, are susceptible to the effects of human activity and are amongst the earliest targets of exploitation through human society.

Virtually all forms of industry in the northern districts of Nizhnii Novgorod were directly related to the forest itself. The major rivers were deep enough to be used for floating timber, which was cut down for local use and export. The rivers were also used to float tar and leather. Local kustar (peasant) craftsmen made carriages, wheels, barrels, troughs, spoons, dishes and shovels; they manufactured wood coal and turpentine. The most systematically damaging form of activity for the forest, however, was the deforestation that gave way to agriculture.

We now turn from nature and economy, agriculture and industry, to Evtuhov's so called local economic rhythms, in nature and culture.

Nature and culture

Multiplicity and diversity of economic structures

The separation between city and countryside in Russia, for Evtuhov, remained partial even up to the early nineteenth century. Life in Nizhnii Novgorod pulsed to the rhythms of the surrounding countryside, as well as to the rhythms of commercial enterprise and those created by the religious calendar. Two points, for her, are critical here: the multiplicity and diversity of emerging economic structures and activities on the territory of this single province, and the constant, active interchange and motion within such.

Economic historians take more or less for granted the basic distinctions between agriculture, industry, trade and commerce. In the Russian experience, particularly in the world of the nineteenth-century province, these manifestly different forms of activity intersected, forming, if not a coherent unity, at least an infinitely connected, integral continuity. This is consistent with the nature and scope of emergence, both culturally and, in this provincial case, economically.

Nizhnii Novgorod province in fact straddled three types of economic space, roughly coinciding with the ecological regions outlined above. First, from the southwest it bordered on the central industrial region that surrounded Moscow. The thick forests beyond the Volga created a second space, where timber and fishing industries predominated. The southeast, third, was mainly agricultural, a final extension of the rich black-soil belt stretching up from southern Russia.

Evtuhov now turns specifically to the issue of land, closely interconnected with the liberation of the Russian serfs in 1861.

Culture and economy in Pavlovo and Sormova

The steelworks of Pavlovo and Vorsma had their own origin myth, as such, which doubles as historical mythology and as a metaphor for the structure of a dispersed "proto-industrial" enterprise. The traditional Pavlovo structure proved remarkably resistant to change, assimilating mechanization and various efforts at factory organization while maintaining a stability of traditional forms. From 1858 to 1895, as such, 75 per cent of workers performed their tasks at home. The Pavlovo region, moreover, had an unusually well-developed network of credit institutions, and it proved a fertile field for experimentation in mutual aid, cooperative organizations, education and artisanal museums.

Sormovo, meanwhile, was a major landmark and world unto itself. The combination of mechanical, iron-smelting, shipbuilding and railroad-engineering and manufacturing employing 8,500 workers made it one of Russia's largest.

A church, a sanatorium, schools for women and men, a canteen, a Sunday school and library, and a hospital were among the services provided, funded in part by a voluntary contribution form the workers' wages. As such, Nizhnii Novgorod industry found resonance in literature: Gorky's *Mother* was for Sormovo what *Sons and Lovers* became for D.H. Lawrence's home town of Nottingham. We now turn to the great fair, Europe's largest at the time.

Bringing together east and west

The largest fair in nineteenth-century Europe, based in the province, brought together east and west: merchants from Bukhara in Uzbekistan and China rubbed shoulders with Armenian traders, and central Russian textile manufacturers. Yet the fair simultaneously represented the culmination of a multitude of local and regional trade networks, and a great festival that transformed the city on the Volga and Oka for two months in the year. Markets for other products dotted the province, moreover, with each market having its particular specialization, depending on local manufacturers.

Education and research, science and culture

"Deep-within" knowledge of things local

In the Nizhnii Novgorod provincial world as such, the gathering of statistical data was characterized by a number of features that, while not by any means unique in the nineteenth century, placed a distinctive mark on the materials collected. Among these, Evtuhov singles out a tendency to conflate numbers with verbal description, with the result that statistical study merged with local ethnography. Moreover, the fact that such information was collected by a cross-section of local intelligentsia, resulted in a "deep-within" knowledge of things local. That was indeed the starting point for a transformative approach to institutionalized research and individual education.

Nizhnii Novgorod in fact was distinctive in nineteenth-century Russia in the intensity of its commerce and enterprise. But this vibrant community of exchange and artisanal production was much more characteristic of Russia at the time than we tend to think. Certainly there can be no more dreadfully inaccurate portrayal of the country, according to Evtuhov, than as characterized exclusively by agricultural production. Yet Marxist-Leninist historiography, with its insistence on a persistent "feudal system", until 1861 portrayed it as such. To the extent, therefore, that the Soviet Union succumbed to Marxism in the twentieth century, so it refuted its own communal grounds, emergent culture and resultant economy and society. Russians rather, from the medieval period onwards, were a people of trade and small-scale production. Everything, in other words, is not what it seems: this dynamic, fluid and infinitely colorful world is the diametric opposite of the ossified and therefore ultimately conflict-ridden social universe of earlier historiographical tradition.

Between art and ethnography

Provincial statistics as an end result, then, might be seen as the art of painting, and thereby researching and educating, with numbers: from the vast production of apparently dry data emerges a vivid social and economic portrait of the province's inhabitants. If the portrait were a conscious creation of the data gatherers, Evtuhov's historical reading a century later brings out features and aspects that may or may not coincide with the concerns of the original counters.

We then turn to local administration, generally, and to the "zemstvo" specifically, for us a form of "integral polity" at a provincial level, serving thereby to align nature and culture, society and economy.

Aligning nature, culture, society and economy in an integral polity

Zemlia: originating locally from the land

A half century after the French social philosopher de Tocqueville's travels in the United States of America whereby he popularized the notions of civil society and civic association, the Spanish writer Dona Emilia Pardo Baza (Valliere, 2001), famous for her introduction of the Russian novel into the Spanish-speaking world, waxed eloquent on the subject of Russian provincial government:

> Among modern institutions, particularly worthy of attention is the "zemstvo" or territorial assembly. Analogous to our Provincial Councils, but of a more liberal nature and a healthily decentralizing spirit. All classes have a seat in the assembly. What effect would it produce in one of our provincial councils to see, alongside the frock coats and topcoats, the jacket with engraved silver buttons of an honest peasant? In Russia

the emancipated serf debates together with his ex-lord. The format of this sort of local parliament is democratic in the extreme: the cities, the laboring class and the landowners elect the representatives, and the assembly devotes itself to the modest but most interesting practical questions of hygiene, health, security, and public education.

Science, culture and the transformative education

We now turn from provincial administration to culture. For Russian nineteenth-century linguist Vladmir Dal, a regional culture, or "cultural nest" may be comprised of a well-tended high school or seminary with gifted teachers, a wealthy public library, a public lecture series in a local university, energetic self-educational circles, the activity of a local scientific society, or indeed their mutual interrelations. Thus the "nests" that he urged his students to investigate included education, the press, theatre, art, as well as socio-economic phenomena.

In fact, one of the key moments in Nizhnii's cultural and intellectual life took place outside the city and even the province, with the founding of Kazan University in 1810, providing a regional centripetal focus and helping to create a local intelligentsia. The Nizhnii Novgorod gymnasium was founded at a secondary level and included instruction in religion, Russian literature, history, geography, maths, physics, natural science, law and languages. It ultimately offered courses in business and accounting as well. Such educational institutions were often closely associated with prominent publications. Gatsiskii, moreover, as we have seen, made the case for decentralization, whereby the provincial life and energy should proliferate alongside that of the capital cities. True progress consisted in the infinitely broad dispersal and dissemination of knowledge, not just concentrated in the "one", but spread among the "many".

Conclusion: mutual development

Activist and catalyst, researcher and facilitator

The central and most self-conscious figure in this process of self-definition of "the idea of the province" embodied in Nizhnii Novgorod, was Alexsandr Gatsiskii's organizing statistical investigations of artisanal production, publishing guidebooks and local histories, promoting the provincial press, and proposing the principle of a "province as a total biography", as if you like the "facilitator", in our terms, of a transformative education, linked to community activation.

Moments of inspiration and glimpses of the transformative potential of this daily facilitation formed an integral part of provincial consciousness. Gatsiskii's future was in fact determined by the timing of his return to Nizhnii Novgorod: the fateful year of 1861, when, as he put it:

> [t]he era of liberation moved certain people to the forefront. At a time of spiritual uplift, of general energy, strength, and hope, everyone who feels God's spark in him abandons his reluctantly inhabited hole and gives himself, so far as his strengths and talents allow, to the common enthusiasm.

Gatsiskii immediately decided to devote the whole of his energies, as activist and catalyst, as researcher and facilitator, to the new challenges facing the Russian provinces.

Gatsiskii then, while a patriot of Nizhnii Novgorod, was an even greater proponent of a more general idea of "province"; *provintsiia* had a good deal to contribute to, and to counterpose, that centralized culture that laid monopolistic claims to represent culture as a whole.

Purveyor of the province to provincial economy

One of Gatsiskii's main points, then, had been that *provintsia* really exists. Evtuhov thereby cites, as general characteristics of Russian development in the second half of the nineteenth century, the growth and expansion of cities, the development of a commercial culture based on retail trade and exchange of services, the emergence of a variety of clubs and organizations, the richness of provincial theatre and the multiplicity of local journals and newspapers, or the appearance of national journals that catered for "middling" tastes in the city and countryside.

In Nizhnii Novgorod, local specifics included the influence of wealthy and respected merchants and, in a province with a particular intensity of religious life, a greater than usual community activism on the part of local clergy. For Evtuhov, moreover, a more useful philosophical notion for conceptualizing the dynamic commercial and cultural world of the Russian provinces belongs to the philosopher Bulgakov who, in his 1912 book, *Philosophy of Economy* (Bulgakov, 2000), proposed that we see the world as household or as economy. Bulgakov spoke of *khoziaistvo* as "the struggle of humanity with the elemental forces of nature with the aim of protecting and widening life, transforming it into a potential human organism".

As such, the Free Economic Society, the Russian Technical Society, the Geographical Society, as research and educational institutions, all played their transformative roles. Overall then, in the provincial Russia to which

Evtuhov has alluded, soil, river, forest provide the value base; enhanced through transformative educators as purveyors of the province; building on such through a provincial diversity of socio-economic structures; effected through a powerful cultural, political and economic zemstvo, ultimately and altogether pursuing mutual advantage.

What equivalent kinds of transformative educational institutions then, are playing a role in relation to your community activation, aligned with awakening integral consciousness, potentially also as innovation driven, institutionalized research institutes? We are now ready to conclude community activation as an integral whole.

CARE to care

In the course of the four volumes on *CARE*/CARE to come, as illustrated in Figure 12.2, we shall be focusing both *functionally* and structurally on integral development as a whole.

In this opening volume, then, we engaged functionally in community activation, with a view to securing livelihoods, building on the vitality of place, thereby initially *CARE*-ing. Structurally, you created community circles, networks and value – socially, if not also permaculture – naturally, initially CARE-ing for integral development. In the next volume we turn to awakening integral consciousness, functionally, and to actualizing an innovation system, alongside such, structurally.

CARE AND CARE
(3)
Innovation Driven Institutionalized Research
Recognize an institutional genealogy

INTEGRAL

Embody Integral Development   *Awakening Integral Consciousness*
Effect Integral Enterprise & Society   Actualize an Innovation Ecosystem
(4)   (2)

DEVELOPMENT

Community Activation
Create a Learning Community
(1)

Figure 12.2 CARE and care.

References

Bulgakov, S. (2000) *Philosophy of Economy: The World as Household.* New Haven, CT: Yale University Press.

Evtuhov, C. (2011) *Portrait of a Russian Province: Economy, Society and Civilization in Nineteenth Century Nizhnii Novgorod.* Pittsburg, PA: Pittsburg University Press.

Lessem, R. (2016) *Integral Advantage: Emerging Economies and Societies.* Abingdon, UK: Routledge.

Lessem, R., Abouliesh, I., Pogacnik, M. and Herman, L. (2014) *Integral Polity: Aligning Nature, Culture, Society and Economy.* Farnham, UK: Gower.

Valliere, P. (2001) *Modern Russian Theology: Bukharev, Soloviev, Bulgakov.* Grand Rapids, MI: William Eerdmans Publishing.

Epilogue

The gene of community activation

Relational, renewal, and reasoned realization paths

Introduction

In this concluding section of this first book on CARE, focused on community activation, we both distil and articulate, in summary, the three paths you may alternately follow, that is "southern" relational, "eastern" renewal or "north-western" reasoned realization, each one with their fourfold integral rhythm, or trajectory: grounding and origination, emergent foundation, navigation and emancipation, effective transformation. As was the case for our previous individual focus on *integral research* (four paths) and *integral renewal* (two paths), you have the choice of which of the now three paths to follow. While the pre-emphasis in your community activation is invariably on grounding, it is with a view to what rhythmically follows (Grounding, Emergence, Navigation, Effect), for each of the three CARE paths – relational, renewal, reasoned realization. Which path then is more or less for you?

First, is the relational path of community activation for you?

Livelihood (G), permaculture (E),
PAR – Participatory action research (N), community building (E)

Relational grounding and origination: livelihood

1   underpinned by ubuntu ("I am because you are");
2   you add natural and communal value;
3   you build up social capital organizationally and/or communally-societally;
4   culminating in communal/organizational common ownership;
5   centred in the securing of livelihoods.

Relational emergent foundation: permaculture

1   you pursue Earth justice following "wild" as opposed to "natural" law;
2   healing the Earth through eco-economic exchange;
3   you build cultural, social and economic worth organizationally/
    societally;
4   participating communally/organizationally in the great work of nature;
5   ultimately centred in permaculture as an interdisciplinary Earth science.

Emancipatory relational navigation: participatory action research

1   you recognize a community's life world (vivencia) in or out of an
    enterprise;
2   enhancing such via people's self-development organizationally/societally;
3   you consolidate upon this by continuously animating the whole
    community;
4   reinforced via action research, in alternating action and reflection cycles;
5   altogether and continuously combining knowledge and action.

Transformative relational effect: community building

1   through socio-economic exchange you provide a value base to a
    community;
2   building on community/organizational culture via justice and
    reconciliation;
3   social business becomes the means of micro or macro navigation for you;
4   making a powerful effect through work or community based democracy;
5   turning markets, marketing, communications into community building.

Second, is the renewal path of community activation for you?

Community healing (G), vitality of place (E)
establish study circles (N), create a world without poverty (E)

Communal grounding/origination of renewal: community healing

1   your community activation is underpinned by nature power;
2   furthered through fusing work and prayer;
3   consolidated upon by combining nature, sprit, science, economy;

4   you ultimately establish a form of communitalism within/without;
5   centred in community healing.

Emergent foundation of communal renewal: vitality of place

1   underpinned by your creating an underlying socio-economic value base;
2   enhanced by your communal relationships, within your enterprise or without;
3   your community and/or enterprise as societally embedded institutions;
4   resulting in trade and accumulation both micro and macro in nature;
5   culminating in the vitality of your particular place.

Emancipatory navigation of communal renewal: study circles

1   you renew participants' genuine interest in individual and collective learning;
2   enhanced by the informal character of your study circles;
3   navigated via your flexible framework to support learning and development;
4   resulting in collective learning, of/through self, community, organization;
5   effected via your institutionalized study circles across enterprise/ community.

Transformed *effect of communal renewal: world without poverty*

1   you begin by creating community to provide the value base;
2   you individually and collectively start the economic engine at the rear;
3   building up towards creating a micro world without poverty;
4   such community building results in the proliferation of social business;
5   ultimately you establish self-sufficiency in the wider community.

Third, is the reasoned path of community activation for you?

Primocracy (G), disclosing new worlds (E)
wealth of networks (N), mutual aid to zemstvo (E)

Grounding community realization: primocracy

1   underpinned by direct democracy;
2   evolving through the evocation of a big restorative picture;

3   amplified by a discursive community;
4   effected via individual and group individuation;
5   serving to actualize a truth quest.

Emergent community realization: disclosing new worlds

1   upheld by virtuous citizenship within your organization or without;
2   enhanced by the cultivating solidarity in your enterprise and/or community;
3   consolidated by disclosing altogether new worlds within or without;
4   involving social, cultural or economic history making, not enterprise;
5   culminating, overall, in fashioning yourselves anew.

Emancipatory community realization: wealth of networks

1   providing underlying commons laden purpose to your community/ organization;
2   enhanced through peer-to-peer-based research and networking;
3   building socially, technically and institutionally via open source connectivity;
4   resulting in institutionalized research networks, communally/ organizationally;
5   culminating with your individual and collective role in an information society.

Transformative community realization: mutual advantage

1   soil, river, forest provide the value base
2   enhanced through purveyors of the province as transformative educators
3   building on such through a provincial diversity of socio-economic structures;
4   effected through powerful cultural, political, economic zemstvo (local government);
5   ultimately transforming education by pursuing mutual development.

Index

Taylor & Francis eBooks

Helping you to choose the right eBooks for your Library

Add Routledge titles to your library's digital collection today. Taylor and Francis ebooks contains over 50,000 titles in the Humanities, Social Sciences, Behavioural Sciences, Built Environment and Law.

Choose from a range of subject packages or create your own!

Benefits for you

» Free MARC records
» COUNTER-compliant usage statistics
» Flexible purchase and pricing options
» All titles DRM-free.

Benefits for your user

» Off-site, anytime access via Athens or referring URL
» Print or copy pages or chapters
» Full content search
» Bookmark, highlight and annotate text
» Access to thousands of pages of quality research at the click of a button.

Free Trials Available
We offer free trials to qualifying academic, corporate and government customers.

eCollections – Choose from over 30 subject eCollections, including:

Archaeology	Language Learning
Architecture	Law
Asian Studies	Literature
Business & Management	Media & Communication
Classical Studies	Middle East Studies
Construction	Music
Creative & Media Arts	Philosophy
Criminology & Criminal Justice	Planning
Economics	Politics
Education	Psychology & Mental Health
Energy	Religion
Engineering	Security
English Language & Linguistics	Social Work
Environment & Sustainability	Sociology
Geography	Sport
Health Studies	Theatre & Performance
History	Tourism, Hospitality & Events

For more information, pricing enquiries or to order a free trial, please contact your local sales team:
www.tandfebooks.com/page/sales